China's
Grand Strategy

China's
Grand Strategy

Weaving a New Silk Road to Global Primacy

Sarwar A. Kashmeri

Foreword by Noel V. Lateef

For Briana,
with admiration.
Sarwar Kashmeri

 PRAEGER®

An Imprint of ABC-CLIO, LLC

Santa Barbara, California • Denver, Colorado

Library of Congress Cataloging in Publication Control Number: 2019015038

ISBN: 978-1-4408-6790-3 (print)
     978-1-4408-6791-0 (ebook)

23 22 21 20 19   1 2 3 4 5

This book is also available as an eBook.

Praeger
An Imprint of ABC-CLIO, LLC

ABC-CLIO, LLC
147 Castilian Drive
Santa Barbara, California 93117
www.abc-clio.com

This book is printed on acid-free paper (∞)

Manufactured in the United States of America

*I dedicate this book to the memory of my dear wife,
Deborah K. Ellis, and to our glorious 40-year love affair.*

*Deborah inspired and encouraged me to write this book,
but tragically, did not live to see it in print.*

*And to the memory of dear brother Zuhair Kashmeri,
impeccable writer, meticulous journalist,
and my best friend for 72 years.*

*He guided me throughout this project, and also did not
live to see it in print.*

Contents

Foreword

With the two largest economies in the world, the United States and China have an outsized impact on the global economy. Indeed, in 2018, China contributed one-third of global economic growth while the United States contributed one-fifth.

Because these two economies are widely viewed as the single most important bilateral relationship, global peace and prosperity will hinge on whether the United States and China can cooperate or, at the very least, compete constructively.

The Foreign Policy Association (FPA) has therefore committed itself in its centennial year to analyzing this vital relationship and is pleased to feature in its Centennial Series this timely book on China's Belt and Road Initiative (BRI) by FPA Fellow Sarwar Kashmeri.

To date, the United States has boycotted the BRI without offering an alternative to it. A far-reaching exemplar of grand strategy, BRI aims to produce an interconnected Eurasian space within which China will play a leading role.

Many countries have engaged with China to leverage Chinese construction capabilities and financial resources to address glaring domestic infrastructure deficits. Kashmeri urges the United States to do the same.

Infrastructure is critical to economic development. It can facilitate or impede trade. According to a report from the American Society of Civil Engineers, the U.S. economy is projected to lose just under $4 trillion in GDP between 2016 and 2025, if necessary investments in infrastructure are not addressed.

Today, 23 million jobs in the United States are tied to international trade. The 2017 *Chicago Council on Global Affairs Survey* found that Americans strongly support international trade, with 78 percent saying international trade is good for U.S. consumers and 72 percent agreeing that it is good for the U.S. economy.

Exports accounted for 12 percent of the U.S. economy, and over 19 percent of China's in 2018. With U.S. exports of goods and services of $120.3 billion in 2018, China is now America's third largest export market. Credible forecasts show U.S. exports to China growing threefold by 2030. Both countries stand to lose if these flows of goods and services are reduced due to trade wars or other kinds of economic confrontation.

One need only look to the plight of American farmers. According to the U.S. Department of Agriculture (USDA), due to the current trade dispute, soybean exports to China plummeted by over 90 percent in 2018. China imports 60 percent of U.S. soybean exports. For many U.S. agricultural crops, China is the principal export market. Once disrupted, agricultural trade relations are not easily restored. U.S. Agriculture Secretary Sonny Perdue predicts, however, that with the conclusion of the current trade dispute, U.S. agricultural exports to China could reach $30 billion annually. The USDA has paid out $7.7 billion so far to help farmers affected by the trade war with China.

This state of affairs brings to mind remarks made at the Foreign Policy Association over a decade ago by Sergey Lavrov, foreign minister of the Russian Federation. Raising the alarm on deteriorating relations between his country and the United States, Lavrov lamented the fact that Russia did not enjoy the extensive trade relations that exist between China and the United States.

More recently, speaking at the Foreign Policy Association's 2019 Financial Services Dinner, World Bank President Kristalina Georgieva observed that trade raises the opportunity cost of conflict. And, in his book, *A Splendid Exchange: How Trade Shaped the World,* William J. Bernstein observes: "World trade has yielded not only a bounty of material goods, but also of intellectual and cultural capital, an understanding of our neighbors, and a desire to sell things to others rather than annihilate them."

The answer to making America or China great again is not to pull each other down. Rather, it is to improve the factors underlying national competitiveness. Infrastructure is one such factor. There is a critical need, acknowledged by both Democrats and Republicans, to revamp America's roads, bridges, railways, and ports. Indeed, President Donald Trump vowed "the biggest and boldest infrastructure investment in American history."

Sarwar Kashmeri raises a tantalizing option that can be exercised only if America can carefully calibrate its relations with China, neither overestimating nor underestimating China's ascension onto the world stage. American engagement with China on the BRI can have a felicitous influence promoting the adoption of international standards and the rule of law. Moreover, if one is not at the table, there is always the risk of being on the menu.

Noel V. Lateef
President and CEO
Foreign Policy Association

Acknowledgments

This book benefits from the advice and in some cases spirited discussion with numerous experts in government, private industry, think tanks, and academia who took valuable time from their busy careers to talk to me about the Belt and Road Initiative and the broader United States–China relationship. Thank goodness, some of them tolerated my barging into their busy lives more than once! This book benefited enormously from these conversations and allowed me to deal with a topic that seemed to be in continuous movement even as I was writing the book.

It goes without saying that any errors and omissions are entirely due to my negligence, not my interlocutors, most of whom are listed here. A few, because of the sensitivities of their position, wished not to be listed by name in this book. To all of them, I owe a very special thanks.

There is no question that my interlocutors were enormously helpful and a source of firsthand information. They inspired me. But the conclusions I came to are entirely my own. It would be a mistake to link any conclusion to a particular interlocutor, unless specifically quoted.

These interlocutors were:

Bonnie Glaser, senior adviser for Asia, and director, China Power Project, Center for Strategic and International Studies (CSIS)

Ching Ching Koh, Group Corporate Communications, OCBC Bank, Singapore

Chuck Hagel, former U.S. Secretary of Defense, U.S. senator (R) Nebraska

Richard Davey, associate director, the Boston Consulting Group

Dhruva Jaishankar, Fellow in Foreign Policy Studies, Brookings India

Dr. Ishrat Hussain, former governor, Bank of Pakistan

Giles Chance, visiting professor, Tuck School of Business, Dartmouth College

Jason Koutsoukis, *Bloomberg News,* Singapore

Lu Yang, postdoc, Tsinghua University, Department of International Relations

Marc Chandler, managing partner and chief market strategist, Bannock-burn Global Forex, LLC

Matt Pottinger, deputy assistant to the president and senior director for Asia, National Security Council, the White House

Mridhula Dharshini Pillay (MFA), first secretary (political), embassy of the Republic of Singapore, Washington, DC

Nisid Hajari, Asia editor for *Bloomberg View*

Pamela Crossley, Charles and Elfriede Collis Professor of History and Professor of Asian and Middle Eastern Studies, Dartmouth College

Parag Khanna, managing partner, Future Map

Paul Haenle, director, Carnegie-Tsinghua Center for Global Policy, Beijing

Raja Mohan, director, South Asian Studies, National University of Singapore

Ravi Velloor, associate editor, *The Straits Times,* Singapore

Raymond F. Greene, deputy director, American Institute in Taiwan

Ryan Haas, David M. Rubenstein Fellow—Foreign Policy, Center for East Asia Policy Studies, John L. Thornton China Center, Brookings Institution, Washington, DC

William Richards, managing partner of WBR Advisors; board member, Jamestown Foundation

During May 2018, I had the good fortune to lead five students from Norwich University (the oldest private military college in the United States) in an independent study course on the Belt and Road Initiative. Their charge was to write a report on 20 of the BRI projects. Four of the students came with me to Singapore to conduct their research. During their work in Singapore, we had many discussions among ourselves and with numerous experts on the Belt and Road Initiative and United States–China relations. The experts included diplomats, senior military officials, journalists, and authors. These discussions sharpened the book's narrative and brought a much-needed Asian perspective to the research. So, I owe these bright students a special vote of thanks and want to acknowledge their initiative, hard work, and contribution to the book: Cadet Staff Sergeant Anthony

Pappas; Cadet Ryan Lechich, AFROTC Det. 867; Cadet Staff Sergeant Marshall E. Harrison; Cadet Corporal Phaleap Taing; and Alec Green.

It was a surprise to find that there is no official or unofficial list of Belt and Road Initiative projects. The Center for Strategic and International Studies was kind enough to make their excellent "Reconnecting Asia" database available to me and Logan Falzarano, a junior at the Lebanon (New Hampshire) High School who used the CSIS database to extract and compile what may be the first comprehensive list of BRI projects. My sincere thanks to Mr. Falzarano for his diligent work and creativity in creating this resource.

Last, but not least, let me acknowledge my gratitude to Noel V. Lateef, president and CEO of the Foreign Policy Association, a legend in the think-tank world. Noel has been a friend and adviser for many years; he was kind enough to serve as a sounding board for many of the ideas that found their way into this book and to write the book's foreword.

The Foreign Policy Association has been my intellectual home for almost three decades. Uniquely, in a world of agenda-driven think tanks, the mission of the FPA today, as it has been throughout its 100-year history, is to serve as a catalyst for developing awareness, understanding, and informed opinion on U.S. foreign policy and global issues. Through its balanced, non-partisan programs and publications, the FPA encourages citizens to participate in the foreign policy process. I can think of no better platform to introduce China's grand strategy and BRI. I was truly surprised and honored when the FPA invited me to write this book as one of its Centennial Publications.

Hilary Claggett pulled this book from concept to reality with her judicious advice. It was sad to see Hilary, who had worked on my two previous books, leave for another opportunity. I was fortunate to have Pat Carlin take over the mantle from Hilary. A meticulous editor, he encouraged me to widen the scope of the book. To both, my sincere thanks. Anna Typrowicz, a good friend who is also a superb professional copy editor, has been the first gate through which this narrative had to make the grade. Thank you also to Shruti Chopra of Westchester Publishing Services and her team for the masterful copyediting.

Finally, a personal note: While I was writing the last chapter, both my dear wife and my loving brother died within three months of one another. It was a catastrophe for me. It was this project that kept me afloat and my mind occupied. In that sense, the book is a marker in my professional life.

ONE

Introduction

In the space of two generations China has transformed itself from one of the poorest countries on Earth to one of the richest. During this process, China has benefited more of its people faster than any country in recorded history. At this rate of growth, within another two generations, China—with its mix of hard-nosed communism and raw capitalism—is destined to become the most powerful and influential country in the world.

But another prize, of even greater significance, is heading China's way: people may begin seeing autocracies as more attractive and beneficial to its citizens than democracies, and may believe that a democratic, liberal world order is not necessarily the best form of government. During the next decades, as scores of countries in Eurasia, Africa, and the Middle East watch China's march to the top of the global league tables, they may surely ask themselves whether becoming rich makes up for relinquishing the rights to vote in a non-rigged authoritarian election and to have a free press. And whether the freedom to criticize their country's leaders makes up for not living a comfortable middle-class life.

I believe that most people who pose these questions will answer them with a resounding "no," and be content to live their lives in a country with a government inspired by China that blends socialism with a market-based economy or, as the Chinese call it, socialism with Chinese characteristics.

China's rise to global prominence is being executed in a three-step grand strategy that began in 1978 with the country opening to the world. That year Communist China's leader Deng Xiaoping famously declared that to get rich is glorious, thus injecting the power of capitalism into the Chinese economy and turning communist orthodoxy on its head. While retaining the ubiquitous iron grip of the Chinese Communist Party over the country, China opened its communist/socialist economy to market forces, industrialized, and became the factory of the world. The results of this dramatic change have been nothing short of breathtaking.

Since the beginning of Deng Xiaoping's reforms, China's gross domestic product (GDP) has risen thirtyfold, and 750 million people have been lifted out of poverty—the most ever achieved during such a short period in recorded history. In four decades, China has gone from the ranks of the world's poorest countries to challenging the United States for the title of the largest economy in the world.

Compiling a list of statistics that illuminate China's growth can be a dizzying experience. Twenty-five years ago, China produced 2 percent of global manufacturing output; today that number is 25 percent, and China is the largest manufacturer and exporter of any country in the world. China has 564 million internet users; over 900,000 cell phone users; more than 12,427 miles (20,000 kilometers) of high-speed rail (meaning trains that travel at 160 miles (250 kilometers) an hour; more billionaires and millionaires than any other country; and, at 84,817 miles (136,500 kilometers), the largest highway system in the world. Such has been the speed of China's transformation that a 40-year-old Chinese citizen will have personally witnessed a time when China's now car-clogged streets were full of bicycles instead, and everyday items such as kitchen shrink wrap had to be imported and were considered luxury items.

By comparison, during the period of China's economic transformation, India, the other Asian giant, with roughly the same population as China, doggedly stuck to its democratic system of government and foundered. As the *Wall Street Journal* has pointed out, people in China live on average nearly a decade longer than their Indian counterparts, and China's per capita GDP is four times higher. China's poverty rate is below 10 percent and falling fast, whereas it is stuck at twice that amount in India.

For that matter, the United States itself does not do too well when viewed against China's ability to increase the lot of its citizens. In its 2016 survey, the Pew Research Center pointed out that between 2000 and 2014, the share of adults living in middle-income American households *fell* in 203 of the 229 U.S. metropolitan areas. A sobering set of statistics for the world's two largest democracies.

The second step of China's unfolding grand strategy was to militarily secure its coastline. Even as China was transforming its economy, it built up its military capabilities. For centuries China's seas were a natural barrier against invasion. But the industrial revolution changed that. As nineteenth-century China's defenses faced in the opposite direction, the industrialized naval might of the West invaded it from the south. China's war junks with their antiquated cannon and noisemaking gongs were no match for the West's industrial navies whose guns demolished Chinese defenses within hours.

Totally defeated and colonized, China then experienced its "century of humiliation," whose numerous depredations included the forced opium addiction by Britain of a large part of the Chinese population, and the forced ceding of Chinese land to Westerners. But such a military misjudgment by China is not likely to happen again.

Today, the biggest threat facing China is the U.S. Navy's fleet of 11 nuclear-powered carrier strike groups (CSGs), each of which packs more power than the entire militaries of most countries. These formidable weapons have maintained America's hegemony in the Pacific since the end of World War II. But that hegemony is now rapidly fading, thanks to China's shrewd military strategy.

With a defense budget that is approximately only a third as big as America's, China knew it could not hope to match the U.S. Navy's global presence and unrivaled strength. China chose instead to focus its smaller defense expenditures on securing its coastline. Today, layers of land, sea, air, and space-based weapons, including nuclear and conventional submarines, medium- and long-range strike aircraft, surface warships, land-based cruise missile installations, especially designed "carrier-killer" missiles, and hundreds of underwater sensors guard the approaches to China's coastline, making it increasingly risky for a U.S. nuclear-powered CSG to sail within 621 miles (1,000 kilometers) of the Chinese coastline in time of conflict. Recognizing the reality that the U.S. Navy's thousand-foot-long carriers will likely not be able to evade Chinese missiles in a future war, the Pentagon in March 2019 began reducing the number of operational carriers by retiring the supercarrier USS *Truman* two decades early in 2024[1]—not a reassuring prospect for the United States or its Asian allies.

After supercharging its economy, transforming its infrastructure, and modernizing its military, China has now begun to execute the third step of its grand strategy—to ally itself with over 70 countries in Eurasia, Middle East, and Africa, in economic-industrial and geopolitical partnerships. China is not following the American formula of constructing a vast military-industrial complex with scores of expensive military bases and treaty alliances. Instead, it is offering to help these countries finance and build roads, railways, ports, bridges, internet connectivity, energy pipelines, and power-generating equipment—the infrastructure that they need to modernize and increase their rate of growth but have not been able to afford. Instead of "forward-deploying" its military around the world, as America has done, China aims instead to forward-deploy its financing, technology, manufacturing, and construction skills to set up connectivity over land and sea with existing and future trading partners, and to lock in multiple sources for its ever-growing need for raw materials and resources.

This web of land and sea connections, that China calls its Belt and Road Initiative (BRI), is the largest infrastructure project in history. Announced in 2013 by President Xi Jinping, with an initial commitment of a *trillion* dollars, the BRI was then incorporated into the Chinese constitution at China's 19th National Congress in October 2017, thus cementing its position as a key foreign policy goal of President Xi.

President Xi always reminds his listeners that China's BRI draws its inspiration from the famous Silk Road of antiquity that served as a trading corridor to connect China to central Asia and beyond. As the old Silk Road grew, cities sprang up in its path to serve as trading emporiums and logistical hubs to keep the ever-growing gusher of commerce flowing seamlessly across a vast region of multiple countries, languages, mountains, deserts, and extreme climates. The key to success of this ancient network was that it was a win-win scenario for all. China grew rich, but so did the cities that acted as intermediaries along the old Silk Road. Now with the BRI, China is building a twenty-first-century version of the Silk Road in which high-speed trains, computers, electronic transactions, multilane highways, and new financial institutions set up by China to specifically help underwrite the BRI will replace the long caravans of ancient times that trudged across Eurasia to barter and exchange goods. What remains unchanged is the win-win formula of the old Silk Road.

Until very recently, the Belt and Road Initiative has not generated much attention in the United States, and there is still little awareness of the BRI and its place in China's grand strategy for global primacy. By placing the Belt and Road Initiative within the concept of China's grand strategy for global primacy, this book breaks new ground.

With a few exceptions, the officials I have talked to tend to pooh-pooh both the concept of the BRI and China's ability to execute the project. Both attitudes reflect the parochial nature of U.S. policy making when it comes to China. Other American officials and experts have described the BRI as an updated version of nineteenth-century colonialism; they believe China intentionally lends more money to countries than they can pay back, and when, as expected, the country is unable to make payments, China swaps the loan for ownership of land and infrastructure, as it did in Sri Lanka.

This attitude is not just incorrect, it is dangerous.

I find myself in the camp of those who believe that the most important foreign policy challenge that the United States will face this century in Asia is accommodating the rise of China as the region's hegemon. In this context, policy makers ought to take the time to understand the many dimensions of the BRI and the irreversible momentum that it has already generated. This understanding might well uncover new channels of cooperation between the two countries, and a more realistic U.S. foreign policy toward China than the failed, so-called, "pivot to Asia" that seemed to have little else going for it but to send more U.S. Marines and warships to frighten China.

The largest part of the BRI is focused on 70 countries in the giant land-mass between China and Europe that contains half of the world's population, 40 percent of its gross domestic product, and 75 percent of its energy resources. Over the next three or four decades, scores of BRI-generated projects will bring gleaming new infrastructure to build up this region, transform its cities, and connect them to each other and ultimately to China.

Witness the transformation of Khorgos, a city on the Kazakhstan-China border. Khorgos's uniqueness lies in the fact that rail traffic from China cannot proceed any farther than the Kazakhstan border unless its contents are physically transferred to another train that can run on the wider Eurasian tracks.

The problem is not dissimilar to one faced by ocean shipments that must be redirected or "transshipped" to get to their destinations. Ninety percent of the world's commerce is seaborne, mostly using containerized cargo ships, the largest of which can sail with thousands of containers on board. Few ports in the world are deep enough to berth ships of this size. Giant seaports along the world's maritime routes that made the capital investment in hardware, technology, and skilled labor to rapidly unload containers from these giant vessels, break them up into smaller lots, and transship them have become rich. Dubai, Singapore, and Rotterdam are good examples.

But transshipment facilities are just the beginning. Once a seaport becomes a major transshipment hub, a natural next step for it is also to serve the myriad other functions required for international commerce: customs formalities, multicurrency purchase and settlement systems, legal and accounting services, duty-free warehouses, ship repair and refueling facilities, showrooms, exhibition halls, and so on. Multiple revenue streams, for instance, have helped Dubai, a sleepy fishing village in the United Arab Emirates, grow into the Jebel Ali Free Zone, one of the world's most successful transshipment hubs, and the biggest port in the Middle East.

To his credit, Kazakhstan's President Nursultan Nazarbayev recognized that with the BRI, China would need a transshipment hub to create a massive land bridge from China to Europe, and what better place to set it up than Khorgos, where the trains would have to stop anyway to change tracks. It was a masterstroke. Today, from mountains and deserts has arisen an entire city that already handles over 500,000 containers a year and is a central cog in the growing trans-Eurasian rail network. It is but one example of what the BRI is accomplishing in dozens of countries.

Or, consider the currently biggest project in the BRI: the China-Pakistan Economic Corridor (CPEC). CPEC is a massive $67 billion project whose objective is to give Pakistan the infrastructure tools, especially the power-generating capabilities that Pakistan's export manufacturers sorely lack, to ratchet up its GDP and increase the average Pakistani's standard of living.

In return, CPEC will reduce the transit distance from the Middle East to China from 8,016 miles (12,900 kilometers) to 1,864 miles (3,000 kilometers) by eliminating the need to use the existing maritime route through the Indian Ocean and the Strait of Malacca. A win-win deal for both countries.

These are just two of the dozens of projects through which China aims to put itself at the center of a throbbing Eurasian continent that is full of gleaming new infrastructure. As the BRI countries get richer, they will consume more of what China produces, as China in turn relies on them for the vast amount of natural resources that the Eurasian landmass contains and that China will need for years to come to maintain its own insatiable need for growth.

The United States will still be a rich and powerful country, but it will undoubtedly wake up one day and wonder how China so outdistanced it in power and global influence.

Just as the West is starting to wake up to the commercial and geopolitical implications of the BRI, it is also just starting to note how Chinese investment and leadership have been reshaping Africa and winning the continent's hearts and minds for decades. Although this book focuses on the BRI, it is worth highlighting China's involvement in Africa to round out the big picture.

Africa's land area is larger than that of China, the United States, India, and all of Europe, *combined!* By 2025, according to the U.S. Chamber of Commerce, Africa's household consumption will total $2.1 trillion, and by 2050, the continent will be home to over 2.5 billion people. Africa is poised to become the largest business opportunity since China embraced capitalism.

In 2000, Chinese companies made a mere two investments in Africa; today, they make hundreds. A recent research project coheaded by Irene Sun for the consulting firm of McKinsey and Company showed already more than 10,000 Chinese firms in Africa. In one African country alone, Nigeria—whose population will exceed that of the United States by 2050—Chinese carmakers, construction material producers, and consumer goods manufacturers are busy jockeying to compete for its vast business market. In Lesotho, "Chinese garment factories make yoga pants for Kohl's, jeans for Levi's and athletic wear for Reebok. Almost all of Lesotho's production is trucked out and packed onto container ships bound for American consumers."[2]

Add the commercial and soft-power benefits of China's African investments to those that will accrue to it from the BRI and one begins to understand that China's grand strategy today aims at replacing the United States as the dominant commercial player and influencer in the world.

Despite the BRI's momentum, China faces several potential obstacles to its continuing successful execution of the BRI. Perhaps foremost among them is the need to manage complex BRI projects in dozens of countries, with cultural, religious, ethnic, and religious populations that are vastly different from the mainly homogenous Chinese. This issue is compounded by China's requirement that its BRI project financing is predicated on the use of Chinese equipment and skilled labor, which has led to protests of projects in countries such as Vietnam, Pakistan, and Sri Lanka, as they contemplate the impact of leasing some of their land to China for 99-year periods, and face the possibility of hundreds of Chinese workers building houses on their land and gobbling up what should be jobs for local people.

Critics of the BRI also accuse China of predatory, colonial practices that, by lending more than a country can afford to pay back (at commercial loan rates), are designed to ensure the failure of the borrowers to pay back the loans. Nonperforming loans give China the muscle to convert the loans to purchase agreements and get ownership of a project's assets and the land underneath. The port of Hambantota in Sri Lanka is a leading example of this criticism of BRI. Unable to repay China in a timely fashion, the government of Sri Lanka had no choice but to convert the loan to a 99-year lease and turn the port and some of the surrounding land over to the Chinese.

Finally, the BRI is a multi-decade project that makes it susceptible to China's list of internal problems such as dangerous levels of air pollution, a slowing economy, and the inequities in job growth and wealth between the rich coastal cities and the largely poor rural communities in China. And then there's the ever-present danger of an unintentional conflict in the South China Sea as President Trump goes eyeball to eyeball with President Xi Jinping over China's claims to almost the entire South China Sea.

These criticisms are serious obstacles and embarrassments for China that if allowed to grow may impact the success of its global ambitions. However, I believe these are growing pains from which China will learn, alter course, but carry on executing its Belt and Road Initiative. After all, China is barely a decade into the execution of its BRI strategy, and less than three decades into its role of superpower. China has much to learn and has demonstrated an uncanny ability to make dramatic changes as its national interests call for them—witness China's 180-degree turn from a socialist to a capitalist economy.

So, a few decades from now, when much of the new Silk Road is in place, the scores of countries it benefits will surely note that it wasn't Western countries, the countries that touted democracy and the liberal world order, that gave them the infrastructure tools and funding to achieve economic success, but instead a socialist-capitalist country that made them rich and gave their people a higher standard of living. Through the BRI—the rebirth of the old Silk Road—China will have won the hearts and minds of a large part of the world the old-fashioned way: by earning them.

Therein lies the ultimate prize for China. The toppling of the belief that democracy is the be-all and end-all of good government and that only through democratic government can countries achieve the best for themselves and their people.

The BRI has already begun to change the world to better align it with China's strategic needs, and it would behoove all of us to get to know what this initiative is all about. Which is why, when the Foreign Policy Association (FPA) asked if I would be willing to write a book to explain the BRI in terms that specialists and lay citizens alike could understand, I could not turn down the request. Especially when the FPA added an unusual challenge to my charge. Would I be willing to peer ahead to the FPA's 150th anniversary in 2068 and forecast what the then China-centric world would look like? It was a unique opportunity to blue-sky and not worry about the brickbats!

The Foreign Policy Association has been my intellectual home for almost three decades. Uniquely, in a world of agenda-driven think tanks, the mission of the FPA today, as it has been throughout its 100-year history, is to serve as a catalyst for developing awareness, understanding, and informed opinion on U.S. foreign policy and global issues. Through its balanced, non-partisan programs and publications, the FPA encourages citizens to participate in the foreign policy process. I can think of no better platform to introduce China's grand strategy and the BRI.

Sarwar A. Kashmeri
West Lebanon, NH
March 2019

TWO

China's Belt and Road Initiative

"Mille vie ducunt hominem per secula sina—All roads lead to China."

So, what *is* the Belt and Road Initiative?

Here's my favorite definition:[1] The Belt and Road Initiative is a $1.3 trillion Chinese-led investment program creating a web of infrastructure, including roads, railways, telecommunications, energy pipelines, and ports, that would serve to enhance economic interconnectivity and facilitate development across Eurasia, East Africa, and more than 60 partner countries. This Chinese initiative was implemented on a bold and unprecedented scale that, in Citibank's words, "seeks to reshape the international trade landscape by promoting enhanced connectivity, trade flows, and investment opportunities between China and numerous emerging and developed markets."

As this book went to press, China's vision was being implemented through scores of Chinese-funded Belt and Road projects under way in over 70 countries that together contain over half of the world's population and a third of its GDP.

The name of the Chinese initiative took time to evolve. Because the BRI was first viewed as an overland "belt" across the Eurasian supercontinent and a maritime "road" across the Indian Ocean to Europe via the Suez Canal, the name One Belt, One Road or OBOR caught on. This later became One Belt and Road, and finally the Belt and Road Initiative, which is now its official name.

The BRI consists of overland economic corridors that are called Belts, and maritime routes that are called Roads. The Belts are a network of roads,

Six corridors: China's Belt and Road Initiative

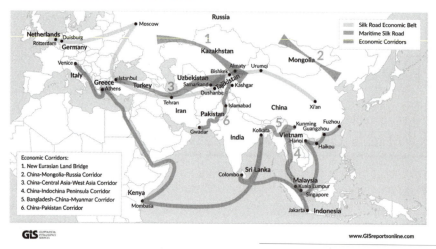

bridges, tunnels, railroad lines, oil and natural gas pipelines, and other infra-structure projects, that connect China with Pakistan, the Persian Gulf, and the Mediterranean Sea, via central and western Asia. The maritime roads connect China's coastal ports to ports in the Indian Ocean and East Africa, and to Europe via the Suez Canal, through projects to build or improve ports and other coastal infrastructure. The Belt and Road Initiative is a money-spinning, commercial tour de force with China at its center.

If success is measured by tangible results, in the first three years (2013 to 2016) since the BRI's start-up, China's total trade volume in the countries along the Belt and Road exceeded $3 trillion, and the initia-tive created $1.1 billion in revenues and 180,000 jobs for the countries involved.

To me, the phrase "The BRI imagines . . ." evokes, better than any other description, the essence of what the BRI is about: an open-ended and bold vision to stitch half the world together with China at the center. It is open-ended in that there is no limit to the number of countries that the BRI includes, or the nature of the infrastructure projects. For instance, besides infrastructure projects, the BRI now has a growing list of Chinese and China-initiated multilateral financial institutions to help finance its projects and will soon have two legal institutions to resolve BRI-related commer-cial disputes.

Jonathan Hillman of the Center for Strategic and International Studies said, only half tongue in cheek, "The BRI is not constrained by geography or even gravity. When announced in 2013, it had two major components: an overland 'belt' across the Eurasian supercontinent and a maritime 'road' across the Indian ocean and up to Europe via the Suez Canal. Since its announcement in 2013, this vision has stretched into the Arctic, cyberspace, and outer space. Countries have signed onto the BRI in places as far-flung from China as Central America."

In fact, the United States itself might be considered to be included in the BRI. After all, the replacement rail cars for Boston's rapid transit system are Chinese, as are the cars now finding their way to the Chicago and Los Angeles Metros! The company involved with these projects is one of the BRI's Chinese vendors.[2] And, until recently, there was serious talk about China building America's first high-speed train that would run between Los Angeles and Las Vegas. China would probably love to describe all these projects in the United States as part of the BRI, but the United States would never accept it. After all, the BRI is aimed at making China great again, not America!

The fact that nothing of this magnitude has ever been tried before means that the rules that guide China's BRI projects are a constant work in progress as China attempts to navigate and reconcile the politics, economies, and cultures of countries as varied as Kazakhstan, Nepal, Hungary, and Greece.

For instance, Kazakhstan's autocratic leader can simply order things done. If an entire new city is necessary to accommodate a BRI project, he can pull the levers to build it, as in fact he has already done at Khorgos, on the China-Kazakhstan border. Then there are Hungary and Greece, parliamentary democracies that are also member states of the European Union. The EU has strict bidding rules for infrastructure projects within its borders, rules with which China is already coming into conflict because Chinese funding for BRI projects usually requires the host country to accept a mainly Chinese workforce, working for a Chinese construction company. Nepal, on the other hand, is a small country sandwiched between India and China, geopolitical and economic competitors. Nepal also happens to be the transit route for Tibetans fleeing from China-run Tibet to India. Tibetan refugees are a very sensitive political issue for China and India, as well as for Nepal, something that must factor into BRI plans.

Extrapolate the political and legal minefields that the BRI faces in these four countries to the 70-plus countries with which BRI is already involved, and one gets some idea of the geopolitical complexities that China is in the midst of navigating as its BRI vision unfolds.

Which is why the definition of BRI at the beginning of this chapter is so apropos.

The phrase "The BRI imagines . . ." also suggests that China recognizes that it expects to make mistakes, to stumble, and perhaps even to fail at times as it implements its vision, but that it expects to correct its mistakes, improve on delivery, and move on the corrected path to its strategic goal of achieving global dominance, the old-fashioned way, by working for it.

In many ways the BRI reminds me of the goal that President John F. Kennedy set for the United States in 1961 to land an American on the moon within a decade. In his address to Congress on May 25, 1961, President Kennedy proposed that the United States "should commit itself to achieving the goal, before this decade is out, of landing a man on the Moon and returning him safely to the Earth."[3] Kennedy had a *vision* of unmatched confidence in America and its leadership. As President Xi Jinping has done, Kennedy was asking Americans to undertake a vast project full of unknowns. In fact, when the president proposed his visionary project, virtually none of the technologies to accomplish a moon landing even existed!

The science of systems analysis that would be required to plan and pull off a project of this magnitude and complexity did not exist; the lunar landing vehicle was the stuff of space fiction; and space navigation and communications, miniaturization of computers, and materials to withstand the scorching heat of reentry had yet to be invented. In fact, when President Kennedy set his now famous goal, America's space endeavors were better known around the world for rockets that blew up, as compared to Soviet rockets that smoothly put Sputnik, the world's first unmanned satellite in space.

A decade later, all that had changed. The United States had invented everything that was necessary for a moon landing, successfully put men on the moon, and returned them to Earth. Executing the unprecedented project left America with leadership in a host of technologies from rugged computers, to space navigation and communication, to the invention of space-age materials. Soon, the inventions for the moon shot flowed down to commercial applications for American homes and businesses. The material—Teflon—that had been invented to protect the reentry capsule from burning up by blazing heat of the Earth's atmosphere soon became a fixture in American kitchens on nonstick frying pans. And the science of systems analysis became a standard tool to plan complex projects and to monitor their execution.

The moon-landing project had just as many detractors and naysayers as does the BRI. But China has leaped into the unknown before; just three decades ago it executed a dramatic about-turn with its economy and won big. Really big.

When, in the late 1970s, Deng Xiaoping, then president of China, steered China out of a staid, planned, lifeless communist economy into the wild, wild world of capitalism, he understood fully the pitfalls and consequences, both known and unknown, that lay ahead for the erstwhile communist country. As they took the plunge, Deng Xiaoping advised the Chinese to "cross the stream by feeling the pebbles," a deep and thoughtful phrase to guide visionary leaders who undertake projects that have few if any precedents. It implies an understanding that unknown paths have unforeseen obstacles that are only revealed when one encounters them on the journey; one needs to be ready to adjust and choose an alternate route to one's goals.

Following this advice and changing directions to avoid pitfalls, China navigated the radical and unprecedented change to its economy with such success that it is about to overtake the United States and become the biggest economy in the world. With that track record and experience, count me in the camp of those who believe that China will overcome the complexities of the BRI by using the discipline and patience it learned during the conversion to capitalism and free markets.

AT THE BEGINNING

The Belt and Road Initiative was officially born on September 7, 2013, on a bright sunlit morning in Astana, the capital of Kazakhstan. Just after 10:30 a.m., President Xi Jinping of China, accompanied by Kazakhstan's President Nursultan Nazarbayev, walked into the conference hall of Nazarbayev University to deliver a speech titled "Promote People-to-People Friendship and Create a Better Future," in which he proposed "to join hands building a Silk Road economic belt . . . to make it a grand cause benefiting people in regional countries along the route."

Xi Jinping reminded his audience that "more than 2,100 years ago, during China's Western Han dynasty (206 BCE to 24 CE), imperial envoy Zhang Qian was sent to Central Asia twice to open the door to friendly contacts between China and central Asian . . . countries as well as the transcontinental Silk Road linking East and West, Asia and Europe." Xi Jinping pointed out that the more than 2,000-year history of exchanges "had proved that countries with differences in race, belief and cultural background can absolutely share peace and development as long as they persist in unity and mutual trust, equality and mutual benefit, mutual tolerance and learning from each other, as well as cooperation and *win-win outcomes*" (emphasis added by author). Xi Jinping also proposed that "in order to make the economic ties closer, mutual cooperation deeper, and space of development broader between the Eurasian countries, we can innovate the mode of cooperation and jointly build the 'Silk Road Economic Belt' step by step *to gradually form overall regional cooperation.* . . . First, to strengthen policy communication. . . . Second, to improve road connectivity. . . . Third, to promote trade facilitation. . . . Fourth, to enhance monetary circulation. . . . [and] Fifth, to strengthen people-to-people exchanges."

In his speech President Xi reminded his listeners that China had done this before with the ancient Silk Road, a connectivity project in the ninth century that had, for hundreds of years, made all the cities it touched, as well as China, fabulously rich. As it was then, so the president of China wanted the new initiative to be a win-win arrangement for all.

Like President Kennedy's speech about getting to the moon, it was a vision statement, meant to inspire. Not a blueprint with detailed construction plans. Unlike Kennedy, Xi Jinping, however, offered no specific date by which the BRI would achieve its goals, though the centennial of the establishment of the People's Republic of China (2049) might yet emerge as a goal.

Seven months later, in October 2013, President Xi launched the second part of his BRI vision, that of a maritime "road," linking China with the nations of ASEAN—Association of Southeast Asian Nations,[4] an increasingly influential group of 10 Southeast Asian countries (Singapore, Malaysia, Thailand, Brunei, Indonesia, Myanmar, Laos, Vietnam, Cambodia, and the Philippines). Again, as in Kazakhstan, history and China's long record of maritime statecraft and trade leadership featured extensively in Xi's speech. (See www.asean.org.)

President Xi told his listeners that the new maritime Silk Road would have a win-win strategic significance for both China and the 10 members of ASEAN, "that since ancient times, Southeast Asia has been an important hub along the historical maritime Silk Road," a commercial sea route stretching from China to the Middle East, that was used as early as the ninth century to trade spices, glass, textiles, and ceramics.

To build the new maritime silk road, China offered to strengthen maritime cooperation with ASEAN countries, making use of "the China-ASEAN Maritime Cooperation Fund set up by the Chinese government." Commenting on Xi Jinping's speech, Yang Baoyun, a professor of Southeast Asian studies at Peking University, wrote that the new route will directly facilitate China's economic development and "like the historical maritime route centuries ago, the new maritime silk road will bring tangible benefits to neighbors along the route, and will be a new driving force for the prosperity of the entire East Asian region."

Besides historians, few in the West would understand the resonance Xi Jinping's references to the ancient Silk Road must have had for his listeners in Kazakhstan and Indonesia. Kazakhstan was the historical beginning of the ancient Silk Road 2,000 years ago. It was the traditional crossing point into central Asia for the first intrepid traders who left China and ventured west to cross the vast, inhospitable regions of Eurasia's great desert, the Taklamakan, emerging after walking 621 miles (1,000 kilometers) of desert into the city of Khorgos, before regrouping and heading farther west.

President Xi Jinping asked his audience to recall that riches beyond imagination resulted as the old Silk Road blossomed. That's what Xi Jinping was asking his audience in Astana to help China re-create—a brand-new version of the Silk Road.

Likewise, in Jakarta, the image of a new version of the old maritime Silk Road would have had a similar resonance for Xi Jinping's Southeast Asian audience. They would recall that Indonesia was a key intermediate port that made the long sea voyage from the Middle East to China possible. In fact, it was in of one of the ASEAN countries—the Philippines—that the maritime trade in Asia underwent a revolution in the sixteenth century. In the Philippines, the ancient international trading practice of barter was replaced with payment by coins. Spanish ships brought large amounts of silver from the Americas to the Philippines. The silver was minted into coins that made large trading transactions far easier.

The new maritime Silk Road that Xi Jinping proposed in his speech was laden with potential new commercial possibilities for ASEAN countries, lying, as they do, between the ports of China and those of South Asia, the Middle East, Africa, and Europe.

Not content with unleashing the largest infrastructure construction project ever, and a $1 trillion (a thousand million!) budget with which to jump-start it, China's next step was to set up a multilateral financial institution to help fund the BRI projects. It was soon evident that the trillion dollars that China had promised to plow into the BRI would be useful to jump-start it, but it turned out to be not nearly enough, as the Asian Development Bank soon pointed out.

The Asian Development Bank estimates that financing Asian countries' infrastructure needs would require $26 trillion between 2016 and 2030, or $1.7 trillion *per year,* to maintain their growth momentum, eradicate poverty, and respond to climate change. (Without factoring in climate change, the infrastructure needs still amount to a massive $1.5 trillion a year.) Clearly, China's start-up financing would need to be augmented by other sources, which, in the world of international development then meant the World Bank and International Monetary Fund (IMF). These Western institutions were set up after World War II to help finance global recovery and keep the world's economies healthy, roles at which the two institutions have done a masterful job.

These institutions, however, are dominated by the West, both in terms of leadership and voting power. "It is an unwritten but firm understanding since the founding of these institutions that the head of the World Bank should be an American, and the head of the IMF a European," says the well-known Singaporean diplomat-scholar, Kishore Mahbubani, who has had a long and distinguished career, including a long stint in New York as his country's UN ambassador, and later as the first dean of the Lee Kuan Yew School of Public Policy at the National University of Singapore. In his provocative book, *The New Asian Hemisphere,* Mahbubani points out that the controlling votes in both institutions are still in U.S. and European hands.[5]

As necessary as these rules may have been after World War II, they are now clearly obsolete, especially if one considers that 88 percent of the world's population lives outside the United States and Europe, and two of the three largest economies of the world (China and Japan) are in Asia.

For China, the World Bank and IMF posed other problems. Both have a bureaucratic bent and are required to consider transparency, environmental, labor, and procurement standards to vet projects before they are considered for funding. Also, their resources for funding infrastructure are limited because both the World Bank and the IMF are involved in a broad range of international development projects, of which infrastructure is just one funding category.

So, China floated the idea of setting up the Asian Infrastructure Investment Bank (AIIB), a new multinational funding institution that would focus on funding only Asian infrastructure projects. Underscoring the Asian focus of the AIIB, the new bank would be headquartered in Beijing, unlike the World Bank and the IMF, which are based in Washington, D.C. The AIIB would fund infrastructure projects throughout Asia, whether or not connected with the BRI, and open its membership to any country in the world that wished to join. However, since infrastructure creation in Asia would, for the foreseeable future, be driven by the Belt and Road Initiative, it was clear that the AIIB was another step in China's strategy to ensure the BRI's success.

Just a couple of decades ago, such an idea from an Asian country would have been considered preposterous and would never have had any chance to get off the ground. Not this time. If anything, the idea of the AIIB was also an unmistakable message of how the world's economic center of gravity was rapidly moving to Asia and specifically to China.

Representatives of 21 Asian nations met in Shanghai in October 2014, to agree to a plan to set up the Asian Infrastructure Investment Bank, and 27 months later, the AIIB opened for business with a capital of $100 billion and 57 founding members. "This is China assuming more international responsibility for the development of the Asian and global economies," the Chinese finance minister said on the occasion.

The bank has continued to grow, and with the approval of the Republic of Lebanon's membership at the AIIB's second annual meeting, held in Mumbai, India, in June 2018, the membership has grown to 87 countries.[6] By comparison, both the World Bank (www.worldbank.org) and the IMF (www.imf.org) were set up in 1944 and have 189 members each.

The AIIB's membership list clearly shows the multilateral nature of the AIIB, while the project list underscores its focus on Asian infrastructure. It is worth noting that in spite of the geopolitical competition between China and India that has prevented India from joining the BRI, the AIIB project list contains a number of Indian projects. This is a tribute to the Asian bona fides of the AIIB.[7]

The establishment of the AIIB resulted in a lot of negative reaction in the United States, where the bank was viewed as a competitor to the U.S.-dominated World Bank. Not only did the United States refuse to join the AIIB, but the Obama administration pointedly asked its closest allies to have nothing to do with it. But, in a show of force that clearly demonstrated China's rising clout and the powerful commercial attraction of the BRI, key U.S. allies simply ignored America's pleas. Led by America's close ally,

Britain, most of America's European allies became launch members of the AIIB at a ceremony in Beijing in June 2015.

The United States was not pleased. Reporting from Shanghai on the occasion of the AIIB's launch, the *Financial Times* observed that, "The creation of AIIB is one of Mr. Xi's signature foreign policy accomplishments. The US opposed the bank and urged western allies not to join, but after the UK broke ranks and announced its intention to join, other countries quickly followed."

Interestingly, this shot across America's bow by its Western allies was fired during the presidency of Barack Obama, who had a far more multilateral bent, and an almost cultlike following in European capitals, as compared to his successor, President Donald Trump!

Even though the AIIB was China's idea, it chose to buy only 26.6 percent of the bank's shares, which gives it veto powers but not control. China's economic heft gives it the right to veto decisions, according to the bank's president, Chinese finance minister Jin Liqun, "This is a major contrast to older institutions such as the World Bank, in which the United States has maintained its veto power by amending the articles of agreement." The AIIB has in fact developed into a truly multinational bank albeit with an Asian focus.[8]

Although China would probably never admit it, the AIIB is also another foreign policy instrument to outflank the United States in Asia by demonstrating China's credibility on the world stage.

The United States has shunned AIIB since it was first proposed, as did staunch U.S. allies Australia, South Korea, and Japan. But since AIIB's launch, Australia and South Korea have also become AIIB members, leaving Japan as the only major American ally in the Pacific that is not an AIIB member.

India, which the United States is now courting as a counter to growing Chinese power in Asia, was also initially skeptical of the BRI. But if the United States believed it was increasingly drawing India away from China, America has had a rude awakening. India has leaped onto the AIIB bandwagon. Of the $4.3 billion lent during the AIIB's two-year existence, around $1 billion went to India. "We're doing things in India with a pace and breadth which is very encouraging. And it shows that any country in Asia, no matter what their diplomatic relations are, is able to engage with and benefit from the work of the AIIB," according to Sir Danny Alexander, vice president at the AIIB and a former British cabinet minister. India's infrastructure needs a major upgrade to keep up with its growth, and it would not be surprising if, over the next few months, India also jumped on board the BRI train.

Besides founding the AIIB, China has focused on creating or joining other multilateral financial institutions to help pump billions of additional dollars to finance the BRI. These include the Silk Road Fund and the New Development Bank, both of which now augment the freshly recapitalized China Development Bank and Export-Import Bank of China.

FOLLOW THE MONEY

"Follow the money" is a well-known dictum in investigative journalism, meaning if you want to know the truth about a person or a situation, track the money involved. By this yardstick, the BRI is not just moving ahead, it is galloping ahead, as evidenced by the multiplication of funding sources for BRI projects, from Chinese state-supported institutions to today's multiple sources of private-sector financing. Besides the World Bank and the Asian Infrastructure Investment Bank, these sources now include money market-based financing instruments such as bonds, as well as international banks. Adding further power to the growth of the BRI is the involvement of advisory and consulting companies, and delivery and logistics firms.

In January 2018, the European website OBOReurope reported that the China Securities Regulatory Commission (CSRC) authorized seven Chinese and foreign companies to issue 50 billion yuan (USD7.5 billion) worth of Belt and Road Initiative bonds through the Shanghai and Shenzhen Stock Exchanges. While BRI bonds offer a new financing mechanism to companies, current limits on how the money generated through the bonds can be used offshore restrict their use, especially in investment portfolios. But assuming the growth of the BRI stays on track, it is only a question of time until these bonds are freely traded around the world and find their way into the portfolios of global wealth managers.

Then, in April 2018, OBOReurope reported that an agreement had been signed between the Shanghai Stock Exchange and the Abu Dhabi Global Market for the establishment of a financial platform dedicated to the Belt and Road Initiative in the Middle East.

In the BRI's rapidly growing trajectory, the trading link between the Shanghai Stock Exchange and the Abu Dhabi Global Market is significant because Abu Dhabi is one of the richest and most progressive of the grouping of seven Middle East kingdoms that are collectively called the United Arab Emirates (UAE). The UAE occupies a central place in trade between China and the Middle East. Many Chinese products are first imported to the UAE and are then transshipped throughout the Middle East, South Asia, Africa, and Europe.

The BRI soon received an endorsement from Michael Taylor, managing director and chief credit officer, Asia-Pacific for Moody's, the international credit rating agency. "Our 'report card' on BRI indicates that overall it generates more positive than negative effects both for China and the recipient countries," he said.[9]

But, the growing involvement of the world's top banks, together with consulting and logistics companies, really underlines the growing attraction of the BRI as an investment vehicle. Project finance, treasury management, currency swaps, and the negotiation of complex multinational laws and regulations are the core competencies of major international banks, and the BRI is nothing if not full of complex international projects!

Here are a few examples of the fast-developing acceptance of the BRI as a potentially lucrative new revenue source by international banks:

- In February 2018, Standard Chartered, a large Asia-based international bank, and China Development Bank signed a five-year memorandum of understanding that will give Standard Chartered access to $1.59 billion to support its BRI lending, having pledged its "long-term commitment" to the initiative.

- Citibank points out[10] that "the Middle East, North Africa, Pakistan, and Turkey (MENAPT) are crucial geographic and economic elements in China's ambitious Belt and Road Initiative (BRI)." Citibank goes on to say that "investment in power, roads, rail, ports, and other infrastructure, coupled with the economic uplift these investments will bring, presents financial institutions, corporations, and sovereigns with a multitude of opportunities. [Meanwhile] much of the finance for Chinese companies taking part in BRI is likely to come from the Chinese government's Silk Road Fund, China's big four state-owned banks (Agricultural Development Bank of China, China Development Bank, and the Export-Import Bank of China), and the Asian Infrastructure Investment Bank." Both Chinese companies and those in MENAPT will also need to access funding from international banks in the form of project finance, syndicated loans, bonds and export credit agency, and multilateral agency support, including that of the Chinese export credit agencies.

- "BRI will be the main driving force behind global economic growth in the next 20 to 30 years," explains Che-Ning Liu, cohead of global banking for Asia-Pacific at another large international bank, HSBC. "It is also one of the main cornerstones of HSBC's global strategy."[11]
- "In the decades ahead, the BRI will also be one of the key driving forces behind China's economy," says Wenjie Zhang, executive vice president and cohead of global banking at HSBC China during the bank's Belt and Road Conference in Beijing. "Clearly it will benefit a lot of Chinese businesses that invest into these countries. It will also benefit local economies and local people who participate in projects along the Belt and Road. Overall, it is going to be a win-win situation for both sides," says Frank Fang, executive vice president and head of commercial banking at HSBC China.[12]
- During a visit to OCBC Bank in Singapore, I was told that OCBC has already provided financing for several BRI projects, including a new water plant in Singapore; coal-fired power plants in Sihanoukville, Cambodia, and Central Java; construction of 920 telecommunication towers across Myanmar; and an alumina refinery in Kalimantan, Indonesia. OCBC is one of Southeast Asia's most conservative banks.
- Deutsche Bank (DB), which has been in China for over 140 years, has presence in around 30 BRI countries. DB is one of the most active international banks to support BRI opportunities. Chinese authorities, including the Ministry of Commerce, applauded a recent transaction, the $225 million credit financing to support a Kazakh oil refinery.

Yet another step in the BRI's achieving global establishment status is the involvement of the world's largest consulting, accounting, and logistics firms, including PwC, KPMG, Deloitte, DHL, and FedEx.

Global financial, manufacturing, and construction companies rely on consulting, audit, and accounting firms such as these for due diligence before committing themselves to participate in new business opportunities. Logistics firms that handle global shipments for their clients have the expertise to negotiate complex import/export laws, tariffs, and customs rules and regulations. Such expertise will be in growing demand throughout the BRI countries as their improved infrastructure sparks a wave of business growth among these countries and between them and China.

In four short years, the Belt and Road Initiative had come a long way. To ensure that the world recognized this accomplishment, President Xi Jinping did what any CEO of a fast-growing enterprise would do. He hosted a massive Belt and Road Forum in May 2017. There, at the Yanqi Lake International Conference Center, north of Beijing, President Xi Jinping gave both the opening and closing keynotes. This paragraph from "The Diplomat's" report from the forum gives a sense of just how far BRI had come in four years.

"The BRF [Belt and Road Forum] served as China's highest profile diplomatic event of the year, culminating in the 30 world leaders [and representatives of 30 more countries] in attendance signing on to a joint communiqué that championed globalization and free trade. 'We reaffirm our shared commitment to build open economy, ensure free and inclusive trade, oppose all forms of protectionism including in the framework of the Belt and Road Initiative,'" the communiqué read in part.

In his keynote address at the BRF's opening ceremony, Xi likewise highlighted the achievements of the [Belt and Road] Initiative so far in a series of bilateral examples. In the three-plus years since rolling out the concept, China has successfully "deepened policy connectivity" with a number of other states and groupings, Xi said. That includes aligning the Belt and Road with the development strategies of the Russia-led Eurasian Economic Union, ASEAN, Kazakhstan, Turkey, Mongolia, Vietnam, the United Kingdom, and Poland. Xi also highlighted a few of the more high-profile projects under the Belt and Road framework. According to Xi, "Total trade between China and other Belt and Road countries in 2014–2016 has exceeded $3 trillion, and China's investment in these countries has surpassed $50 billion."

One final point in describing the Belt and Road Initiative: No business plan is complete without a carefully thought-out public relations campaign to supplement the plan's business objectives. Corporations head to Madison Avenue in New York to help craft a strategy to illuminate their business plans. China decided to use its own homegrown public relations arm—the Confucius Institute—to supplement President Xi Jinping's carefully cultivated BRI vision of a generous, gentle, human, win-win initiative by the Chinese government.

The Confucius Institutes follow a path laid out years ago by major Western powers. When I was growing up in Bombay (now Mumbai), India, major Western countries had (and still have) cultural centers in key Indian cities to capture the hearts and minds of Indians. The centers are essential arms of countries' foreign ministries or state departments. The United States Information Service, the British Council, the Alliance Française, and Germany's Goethe Institute are some of the best-known examples of these centers.

All these centers, with the notable exception of the United States Information Service that was regrettably disbanded as an economic move, still exist. All of them serve as central communication points to try and win the hearts and minds of the host countries' citizens. For instance, the website of the American Alliance Française (AFUSA) describes itself as "the place to learn and immerse yourself in all things French. We are a dynamic network of local, independent chapters passionate about promoting the French language and celebrating francophone cultures."[13]

With the advent of the Belt and Road Initiative, which symbolizes China's debut as a great power, China has begun to follow a similar path by making its already existing Confucius Institutes an important supporting structure for explaining the cultural and moral rationale behind BRI. Here's the official line from the institute's website, "Confucius Institute (Chinese: 孔子学院; pinyin: Kǒngzǐ Xuéyuàn) is a non-profit public educational organization affiliated with the Ministry of Education of the People's Republic of China, whose aim is to promote Chinese language and culture, support local Chinese teaching internationally, and facilitate cultural exchanges."

BDNews24.com, the Bangladeshi news portal, does an even better job of explaining the rationale behind the Confucius Institute from an Asian perspective: "As China came out of its shell to be an economic power with global ambitions following the launch of the Belt and Road Initiative (BRI) by President Xi Jinping, there was a crying need to make people across the world aware of China, the Chinese language and Chinese culture. The isolationist policies of the earlier Maoist era had made China a strange place and its people seem inscrutable. This needed to be corrected and corrected urgently, given the feverish pace of China's expansion."[14]

In the last 15 years, the March 28, 2019, *Wall Street Journal* reported, the government of China opened over 100 Confucius Institutes at U.S. universities for a cost exceeding $158 million. The universities included Emory University and the University of California, Los Angeles. Through these

U.S. institutes, more than 500 classrooms teach American students in kindergarten through 12th grade.

Interestingly, in its article, the *Wall Street Journal* also reported that a U.S. Senate panel recommended abolishing more than 600 Chinese government-funded cultural and language programs at U.S. schools and universities unless Beijing allows equal access to American public diplomacy efforts.[15]

Lest anyone still doubts the central role of the BRI in China's grand strategy, four months after the Belt and Road Forum, at the 19th National Congress of the Communist Party of China (CPC) in November 2017, President Xi Jinping engineered an amendment of the Chinese Constitution to include the Belt and Road Initiative as one of China's major future objectives.

At the same conference, the CPC removed the constitution's two-term limit on the Chinese presidency to allow President Xi Jinping to keep his office for as long as he wishes. This ensures that the BRI will continue to be personally directed by the same president of China throughout its implementation. Although the BRI has no publicized formal end date, 2049 seems a likely one, being the 100-year anniversary of the founding of the People's Republic of China.

As Mr. Jagannath P. Panda, research fellow at Institute for Defence Studies and Analyses, New Delhi, has shrewdly observed, "The BRI's inclusion in the CPC's amended constitution is a significant development since the international community mostly views the initiative as an economic strategy that is linked to China's external engagement policy, and less of a 'political' proposition. No matter how minor this amendment might appear to be, it signifies a 'Chinese state strategy' in the making, both in the domestic and international contexts."[16]

Mr. Panda's observation offers as fine a place as any to segue from a general discussion of the BRI to some of its key strategic dimensions.

THREE

BRI—A Marshall Plan on Steroids

"If ignorant both of your enemy and yourself, you are certain to be in peril."

—Sun Tzu, *The Art of War*

Until a few months ago, the Belt and Road Initiative generated barely a ripple in the U.S. media. Smug smiles bordering on contempt were on display in conversations with foreign policy experts at the very idea of such a vast globe-spanning project being successfully executed under China's leadership. And the proposition that the BRI could ever pose a direct challenge to America's power and influence in Asia, and potentially around the world, would until recently have drawn raised eyebrows and knowing smiles in Washington's foreign policy circles. A description of the BRI as a part of China's grand strategy would have met with outright laughter and by and large still does.

LESSONS FROM THE EURO?

This attitude of polite contempt at the thought of anyone other than the United States being able to conceive, much less execute, a game-changing geopolitical initiative reminds me of similar American attitudes during the introduction of the European single currency, the euro. Even though the euro was about to become the currency of over 300 million people in Europe,[1] as late as a year before the euro's launch, most Americans had not even heard of it, and many of those who had simply could not believe that Europeans would voluntarily give up one of the most cherished symbols of a country's sovereignty—its currency. Germany without its cherished deutsche mark, or France without its franc. *Mon dieu!*

Business often took me to Europe during the months preceding the introduction of the European single currency. There, every newspaper was full of headlines that spoke to the euro and what it might or might not mean for the European Union (EU) and the world. It was the biggest item of news in cities such as London, Paris, Berlin, and in the other countries that were about to ditch their currencies for the euro. But back in the United States, there was almost no mention of these transformational developments.

I remember then Undersecretary of Commerce for International Trade David Aaron's keynote speech at a conference that my then company, Niche Systems, Inc., and the World Affairs Council in Washington, D.C., had organized at the U.S. State Department on the business policy implications of the euro. In his prepared remarks, he summed up the largely negative skeptical view of the euro in the United States by telling the audience that, to the best of his knowledge this was the *first* conference to be held in Washington on the euro's potential impact on U.S. business and public policy. This was on the eve of the launch of a currency that could in the future pose a serious threat to the United States. It could affect the dominance of the U.S. dollar in global currency markets and would have immediate impact on the sales, marketing, and pricing strategies of American companies, and require modifications to their accounting systems software.

The euro has not displaced the U.S. dollar, but today, along with the U.S. dollar and China's renminbi, it is one of the three most important currencies in the world. Whether it ever replaces the dollar is open to debate, but there is no debate that the euro is one of the world's most consequential currencies, and it is held in the foreign currency reserves of every important central bank, including China's.

I have often wondered why American officials pay so little attention to developments in other countries that could have a serious impact on the United States. The conclusion I have drawn is American hubris. And so it is with the Belt and Road Initiative.

Besides the importance of the BRI in China's strategy, it is critical to keep being reminded of the practical economic and commercial underpinnings of the Belt and Road Initiative. The BRI already encompasses hundreds of infrastructure projects in 70 countries, projects that will absorb China's growing surplus of skilled manpower and manufacturing capacity. These are the skilled resources that helped design and build China's twenty-first-century infrastructure of roads, high-speed rail, bridges, dams, airports, tunnels, and fiber-optic internet connectivity.

Now as this construction binge matures and slows, China will not need as many of these resources. Rather than reduce its valuable infrastructure-building capabilities, China is deploying them throughout the BRI countries, to help these countries in turn build their own infrastructure, which will then allow China's BRI partners to fuel their economies through export-led growth, and to raise their standard of living, just like China has done.

Together with helping the Belt and Road Initiative countries construct the infrastructure that they need, the BRI increases the odds that future infrastructure replacement, repair, and maintenance budgets of these countries will be spent in China. As the Belt and Road Initiative countries ratchet up their economies with their new infrastructure, and become richer, China's involvement in the countries and the expanding middle class in those countries will create new markets for Chinese exports. This will also put China at the head of the line to gain access to the raw materials of those countries, thus feeding China's future growth.

With China at the center of all this connectivity, the BRI has already started to create a vast symbiotic commercial belt that will increasingly speed the flow of goods, services, and finance between BRI partner countries and China, enriching both sides and thereby beginning to fulfill President Xi Jinping's promise of re-creating a win-win model of the old Silk Road with the Belt and Road Initiative.

THE MARSHALL PLAN

While President Xi Jinping's carefully choreographed Chinese comparison of the Belt and Road Initiative to the ancient Silk Road is at the center of China's public relations efforts, another more recent comparison may be easier for Americans to relate to: the 1948 U.S. Marshall Plan, America's financial aid package to help rebuild Europe after World War II.

World War II was a cataclysmic conflict that smashed Hitler's Germany into submission to the Allied forces, led by the United States. As ThoughtCo. describes it, "The six years of World War II took a heavy toll on Europe, devastating both the landscape and the infrastructure. Farms and towns were destroyed, industries bombed, and millions of civilians had been either killed or maimed. The damage was severe, and most [European] countries didn't have enough resources to help even their own people."[2]

The United States, in contrast to both the other Allied nations and Germany, was not just intact; it was, literally, the last country standing. In the four years after America was drawn into the war by the Japanese surprise attack on Pearl Harbor in 1941, the United States had converted its huge manufacturing and industrial capacity to wage total war, with the result that at the end of the war, while much of Europe was destroyed, America was at the height of its industrial manufacturing capacity. Its factories spewed out veritably unending numbers of tanks, ships, artillery, munitions, airplanes, and all the other instruments of total war. Responding to the Japanese attack of December 1941, President Franklin Roosevelt had promised to convert America into "the Arsenal of Democracy," and he had delivered, in spades.

Leading American strategists and politicians recognized that the mismatch between America's wealth and Europe's poverty, if left unattended, would ultimately rebound to hurt the United States' economy and that of Europe. Besides, the Soviet Union, an ally in the war, was now aggressively propagating its communist brand of government throughout Europe. In fact, a growing part of Eastern Europe was already under Soviet control, and communist parties were gaining ground in France and Italy. As Britain's wartime prime minister Sir Winston Churchill memorably put it, "from Stettin in the Baltic to Trieste in the Adriatic an iron curtain has descended across the Continent." Something had to be done to correct this state of affairs.

Fortunately for America and for Europe, the United States was then a country with leaders who were able to dream big dreams, forge bipartisan consensus, and use government institutions to make their dreams a reality. Among these postwar American giants was General George C. Marshall who, as the wartime military's Chief of Staff, had engineered the defeat of Nazi Germany. He was now the U.S. secretary of state.

Marshall conceived a brilliant plan, and the United States Congress passed legislation to help Europe rebuild with American financial assistance. The aid plan within the legislation (soon dubbed the Marshall Plan after its founder) would provide a gift of $15 billion (equivalent to around $110 billion today) over four years to both European Allies and Germany to help them rebuild their shattered countries. It was a magnanimous, farsighted act by the United States that could easily have been described with the phrase, "win-win," the words President Xi Jinping used to describe the Belt and Road Initiative.

The Marshall Plan "gave" reconstruction money to the Europeans, not in the form a check that they could cash, but as a credit to use for purchases to rebuild their countries. With one proviso: The aid money had to be spent in the United States. Under the legislation, no money would flow across the Atlantic. Instead, Europeans would buy from American companies against the Marshall Plan's credit, the American companies would receive payment from the U.S. Treasury, and the dollars would ultimately flow to U.S. workers in the form of their payroll checks.

American factories that produced tanks and artillery would convert their assembly lines to produce consumer and construction products to help Europeans speed up the rebuilding of their countries and economies. And the factories and workers that had made America the "arsenal of democracy" would now build homes, as well as produce an increasing number of luxury goods that a growing American middle class would want in what became a new American gilded age. The faster Europe got on its feet, the faster would be the conversion. It was as elegant a solution as it was far-thinking and magnanimous.[3]

Not only did the Marshall Plan help U.S. industry convert its manufacturing capacity to peacetime uses, it also helped U.S. companies to set themselves up in Europe to be closer to their customers. In time, as European countries rebuilt their economies, European companies would in turn invest in America, thus setting up a commercial relationship that has continued to enrich Europeans and Americans ever since. In 2018, according to the American Chamber of Commerce in the EU's annual survey of jobs, trade, and investment between the United States and the EU, the transatlantic economic relationship was responsible for one-third of global gross domestic product, $5.5 trillion in commercial sales, and 15 million jobs. Quite a return on an initial investment in 1945 of $110 billion.[4]

Riding on the momentum of the Marshall Plan, the Atlantic allies would soon create the North Atlantic Treaty Alliance (NATO) and the multilateral institutions that have guided, and continue to guide, the global economy, including the World Bank, International Monetary Fund (IMF), and the World Trade Organization (WTO). This collection of institutions, led by the United States, formed the foundation of what soon was labeled the liberal world order.

Until China's recent rise, a challenge to this liberal world order led by the United States was inconceivable; after all, the United States had the largest GDP in the world and, with its European Union trade connections, was the fastest-growing region. No other country came close to straddling the world as an economic and military colossus as did the United States. Until now that is.

Today, China is poised to become the largest economy in the world. Indeed, using purchasing power parity (PPP), one of two ways in which economists measure a country's gross domestic product, China already is the world's top economy. And Asia, with China in the lead—not the West with America in the lead—will be the world's engine for economic growth in the twenty-first century. "Chinese economic power will dominate the 21st century," was the consensus of a 2017 discussion at Britain's influential Royal Institute for International Affairs (popularly known as Chatham House). China will likely dominate the coming decades, achieving global dominance through economic means, while the projection of American power through military means—and that of Europe through social democracy—will become less pertinent in what one panelist at the London conference called the "Eurasian Century."[5]

If the previous chapter's description of the long-term strategy of the Belt and Road Initiative reminds readers of the Marshall Plan, it should. There are differences, of course. Instead of $110 billion, the BRI plans to invest $1,000 billion. Instead of a four-year plan, the BRI remit spans decades. Instead of a basically similar grouping of countries in western Europe that were the targets of the Marshall Plan, China aims to stitch together a wide swath of the world, from eastern China to central Asia, Western Europe, and Africa. Perhaps a Marshall Plan on steroids might be a more apt analogy!

The comparison of the Belt and Road Initiative to the Marshall Plan could easily go further. The venerable Western multilateral financial institutions—inspired and led by the United States—that were established in the wake of the Marshall Plan will now be joined by new ones, inspired by and tailored to China's Belt and Road initiative. These include the Asian Infrastructure Investment Bank, the Silk Road Fund, and the Asian Investment Bank.

Chinese companies are establishing themselves in Eurasia and Africa using funding from the Chinese government's $1 trillion BRI pool to launch projects and to draw private capital from banks, investment firms, and, increasingly, capital markets, developments that mirror what happened in the wake of the Marshall plan.

In fact, the more one digs into the BRI as the driver and underwriter of China's grand strategy, the more conceptually appropriate the comparison to the Marshall Plan becomes. After all, the American-led world order began when the United States economy was the largest in the world. Now, with China's imminent rise to the largest economy in the world, the creation of a China-led world order is under way. And, just as the Marshall Plan triggered the transatlantic economy, the Belt and Road Initiative is set to trigger a Eurasian-African economy centered on China. Western critics of BRI are quick to point out that the big difference between the Marshall Plan and the BRI is that the former "gave away" money while China lends at market rates. A distinction that dozens of BRI-allied countries seem to have shrugged off.

ALLIANCES

American officials have always maintained that its constellation of alliances around the world, especially those in Europe, give the United States an unbeatable edge in comparison to China, as exemplified by U.S. Secretary of Defense Ash Carter's assertion at the 2017 Shangri-La Dialogue, the top Asian Defense conference held annually in Singapore, that Beijing is "erecting a great wall of self-isolation."[6] The *South China Morning Post* took a different tack from Secretary Carter when it observed that states engage in military alliances to protect themselves against threats from other states, whereas China doesn't need alliances for survival.

Today China is the second largest economy in the world, and a nuclear power. China has become, as Deng Xiaoping said, a pole itself. An invasion into the Chinese mainland by any country is next to impossible. As the late German Chancellor Helmut Schmidt said, "You [China] are big enough and you will be able to stand alone."[7]

I do not believe the U.S. establishment's proposition that America's alliances give it the competitive edge against China for two reasons.

First, America's strongest allies deserted it when push came to shove, both in conflict and in commerce. For instance, during America's 2003 invasion of Iraq, the country found itself virtually alone. Some of its biggest allies, such as France and Germany, wanted nothing to do with a war they considered illegal because the United Nations had not authorized it. Then in 2017, as noted earlier, when the United States did not want its allies to join China's Asian Infrastructure Investment Bank because it viewed the AIIB as a direct competitor to the American-led liberal world order and two of its key institutions (the International Monetary Fund and the World Bank), virtually every ally deserted the United States—including Britain, its supposedly closest ally.

Second, the American proposition that China has few allies does not make any sense because it is devoid of reality. After all, China is the largest exporter in the world and already has more commercial alliances than does the United States. As Parag Khanna, foreign affairs expert and best-selling author, has repeatedly pointed out, China isn't a backward, isolated socialist economy; it is in fact a country that's the top trading partner of *twice as many countries* [emphasis mine] as is the United States.[8] But these relationships are *commercial partnerships,* not military alliances of the kind that the United States counts in its quiver as giving it the edge over China. The dozens of additional alliances that China will generate through the Belt and Road Initiative will also be of the same ilk, commercial partnerships rather than the American model of expensive defense treaty-based global commitments to protect countries with whom the United States also does business.

If one were to post America's alliances on a balance sheet against China's existing commercial allies and those that will emerge from its Belt and Road Initiative, most of America's alliances would post as liabilities and China's as assets. The United States has 40,000 military personnel in Japan and 35,000 deployed in South Korea,[9] and has U.S. Marines in Australia. These and many other countries fall under the paid-for defense umbrella of the United States. And then there is the North Atlantic Treaty Organization (NATO), the most expensive U.S. alliance of them all.

Consider this excerpt from a February 2017 *Huffington Post* column: "The U.S. plans on filling Eastern Europe with thousands of troops along with vehicles and weapons to equip an armored combat brigade. That will require a special budget request of $3.4 billion for next year. Uncle Sam may be bankrupt, but nothing is too expensive for our pampered European allies, who enjoy greater wealth while spending far less on the military."

The United States committed to defend Europe through NATO in 1949, against a powerful and aggressive Soviet Union. Underwriting Europe's defense then—when Europe was shattered and poor—made sense. But today, the Soviet Union has imploded, while the European Union is the richest group of countries in the world. There is no reason why Americans taxpayers should still foot the bill to defend Europe, especially when the European countries together spend far more on defense than Russia does, and two of the them, Britain and France, are nuclear powers.

Now contrast this with China's alliances. Except for the small Chinese outpost in Djibouti, Africa, China has no other military commitments that complicate its life. Unlike the trouble spots in the world in which the United States claims it needs to be involved, China is not encumbered with the baggage that comes with calling itself "leader of the free world," as America does. China's alliances are focused on making money and letting its partners make money.

Perhaps it is time to update the definition of alliance to better reflect the realities of the twenty-first century. Just as the post-Deng Xiaoping world had to tailor the definition of socialism to become socialism with Chinese characteristics, might it not be time to call China's commercial partnerships "alliances with Chinese characteristics"? After all, who is to say that the BRI partners such as Sri Lanka, Pakistan, and Vietnam will not in the future also take on some limited characteristics of a military ally when their national interests require it—just as America's treaty partners split company with the United States when their national interests required it.

In my opinion, the United States should be seriously pondering the definition of "alliance" to avoid a misleading strategic mindset. After all, the United States is a capitalist country that will soon be vastly outnumbered by all the alliances with Chinese characteristics.

If the 70-country Belt and Road Initiative is as successful as China intends it to be, and there is no reason why it shouldn't, China will wind up with far more allies and partnerships than the United States has today. China will then have placed itself at the center of a wide belt of mutually beneficial ties that will continue to generate commerce and goodwill for decades, without the long-term liabilities that the United States took on after its Marshall Plan. If the Marshall Plan was America's masterstroke of the twentieth century, the BRI will one day be considered China's masterstroke of the twenty-first century.

Although unquestionably, current and future trade and commercial ties (and perhaps some military ties on the distant horizon) are prime drivers of the Belt and Road Initiative, China also aims to address another significant strategic objective through the BRI. It is an objective that poses a potent threat to China's long-term security and growth, and is an outgrowth of geography. This is the Malacca Dilemma.

THE MALACCA DILEMMA

For China's spectacular growth to continue, it will need secure and continued access to imported energy resources, especially oil, to power its economy, and will also need secure channels for its imports and exports.

As a RAND Corporation report[10] points out, China's energy requirements will equal that of the United States by 2020. And despite China's growing use of sustainable energy resources, oil will continue to power 20 percent of China's energy requirements for the foreseeable future.

According to the RAND report, "Without new discoveries, . . . China's oil import dependence will increase from around 11 percent in 1996 to almost 60 percent in 2020. (The share of China's natural gas import dependence will also increase to at least 30 percent by 2020.) Without the discovery of substantial new reserves or a decision by the Chinese government to backtrack from its policy of market reform and restricting imports, these statistics indicate that China's reliance on foreign sources of oil and gas will continue to grow over the next two decades." Most of these energy imports, including 87 percent of its oil, come from the Middle East, Latin America, and Africa over the well-established, centuries-old maritime routes through the Indian Ocean to the ports on China's eastern seaboard.

By a quirk of nature, the shortest sailing route between the Indian Ocean to the Chinese ports is through the Strait of Malacca, a narrow shipping lane that lies between the Malay Peninsula and the Indonesian island of Sumatra, then exits at Singapore into the South China Sea, and continues its way via China's major trading ports to the Pacific Ocean. Over 60 percent of China's commerce passes through this narrow waterway that is 500 miles (805 kilometers) long, but is only 1.7 miles (2.5 kilometers) wide at its narrowest point off Singapore. China is the largest exporter of finished goods in the world, and the second largest importer, and almost all of China's external trade is seaborne; shipping lanes are the lifeblood of China's economy.[11]

The Strait of Malacca is China's jugular because it is what naval strategists call a "choke point," a critically important narrow sea route that would be easy to block in time of conflict. China's overreliance on the Strait of Malacca for over half of its commerce and future oil imports is known, in a phrase coined by China's former President Hu Jintao, as the country's Malacca Dilemma.[12]

The Strait of Malacca exits into the South China Sea and is the primary route used for commerce and energy supplies from the Middle East and Africa, not just to China, but also to Indonesia, the Philippines, Taiwan, and Japan.

In addition, geologists believe that the South China Sea itself may contain more oil reserves than any other area in the world but Saudi Arabia[13]— an important reason why China claims ownership to almost virtually all the South China Sea, including the shoals and islets within it. These ownership

Table 3.1   China's Top Crude Suppliers, 2016

Country	Volume (1,000 barrels/day)	Percentage of Imported Crude Oil
Russia	1,009	13
Saudi Arabia	847	11
Angola	773	10
Iraq	641	8
Oman	640	8
Iran	531	7
Venezuela	320	4
Brazil	288	4
Kuwait	278	4
UAE	251	3
Others	2,029	27
Total	**7,607**	**99**

Numbers may not equal 100, as figures have been rounded.

Source: Author created based on information from Chapter 2, "Energy Demand and Supply in China," from the Rand Corporation's report "China's Quest for Energy Security," www.rand.org/pubs/monograph_reports/MR1244 .html.

claims are disputed by several countries including Japan, the Philippines, Vietnam, Taiwan, Borneo, and Indonesia.

If the geologists' forecasts of the oil reserves are correct, South China Sea ownership and exploitation of the energy deposits under it would be one way for China to lessen (but not eliminate) its dependence on the Strait of Malacca.

With so much oil and commerce transiting through the South China Sea and the potential of rich resources buried in its waters, the claims and counterclaims for ownership, and the insistence by the United States that its naval presence in the South China Sea is necessary to defend America's and its allies' interests in Asia, the South China Sea has become a ticking time bomb—perhaps the hottest of the world's hot spots, as the United States and China jockey for dominance. All of which make it critically important for China's grand strategy both to militarily dominate the South China Sea and its eastern seaboard, and to reduce China's existential reliance on the Strait of Malacca.

DOMINANCE OF THE SOUTH CHINA SEA

My own conversations with naval strategists over the last two years have convinced me that China is already the militarily dominant power in the South China Sea. That information also became public as part of the written testimony submitted by then U.S. Pacific Command Chief Admiral Harry Harris in April 2018 to the U.S. Senate Committee on Armed Services. His message to the U.S. senators was unambiguous: "In short," Admiral Harris wrote, "China is now capable of controlling the South China Sea in all scenarios short of war with the United States."[14] War with an antagonist that has the nuclear capability to destroy the United States being highly unlikely, the admiral might as well just have said, "China is now capable of controlling the South China sea in all scenarios" and left out the qualifying second half of the sentence!

China has established hegemony in the seas around it by following two intertwined strategies: modernizing its armed forces while continuing to strengthen and militarily enforce its claims of ownership to virtually all the islands and reefs in the South China Sea, despite counterclaims from many of its neighbors.

As I pointed out in the introduction to this book, the United States relies mainly on its nuclear-powered carrier strike groups (CSGs) to project American power around the world. The United States Navy describes a CSG "as composed of roughly 7,500 personnel, an aircraft carrier, at least one cruiser, a flotilla of six to 10 destroyers and/or frigates, and a carrier air wing of 65–70 aircraft. A CSG is the largest operational unit of the United States Navy and comprises a principal element of U.S. power projection capability."[15] The United States has 11 CSGs; no other country has even one.

U.S. Navy lore has it that U.S. aircraft carriers and their accompanying warships can leave U.S. territory, disappear into the vast Pacific Ocean, and arrive on China's doorstep undetected, but the reality today is very different. As mentioned earlier, China has already deployed a combination of sophisticated maritime sensors; drones that can stay aloft for months; specialized carrier-killer weapons; and an array of rocket, missile, and naval defense technology that now make it virtually impossible for a U.S.

nuclear-powered CSG, the cornerstone of U.S. global dominance, to operate within (621 miles) 1,000 kilometers of the Chinese coastline.

Admiral Harris's testimony simply underscored what some U.S. naval experts have believed for many years—that the 100-year reign of aircraft carriers in combat is over, especially against a technologically advanced country such as China.[16]

Although it is certainly true that the United States continues to develop increasingly advanced defense technology to protect its CSGs, the odds are still overwhelmingly on the Chinese side. As an example, America's most sophisticated aircraft carrier, the Ford class carrier, that is entering service in the U.S. Navy costs approximately $13.5 billion, while the cost of the most sophisticated Chinese anti-carrier missile, the DF-26, is approximately $11 million. That means China can build 1,227 anti-carrier missiles for every carrier the United States builds.[17]

These odds do not even consider that each of China's anti-carrier missiles is fitted with multiple, individually targetable warheads that would zoom into a carrier from multiple directions at supersonic or—given China's recent missile advances—hypersonic speed. The odds of an American carrier surviving an attack with 50 or 100 such missiles coming at it simultaneously in a conflict with China are, to be generous, remote.

How has China been able to accomplish this maritime military tour de force when its defense budget of approximately $171 billion is about a fourth of America's huge $824 billion defense budget? The answer is that China has focused its military budget on defending its coastline and aiming for military dominance of the seas and archipelagos that must be navigated by U.S. forces seeking to attack China from the Pacific Ocean, from China's east.

China does not have any ambition (at least not yet) to militarily dominate the world. Therefore, the People's Liberation Army's (PLA) military modernization plans launched in 2006 are geared to transform the PLA into a force capable of conducting joint operations and fighting and winning "informatized local wars," regional conflicts defined by real-time data-networked command.[18] These would be high-intensity, fast-moving, technology- and information-centric wars in China's backyard. Here are two examples from the Pentagon's Annual Report on China's military power.

China has re-organized its air and naval units to counter what it sees as the primary threat to its security: a potential attack from the United States which would come from the east. Almost all of China's naval units are based along its east coast and are positioned to provide overwhelming firepower to dominate the seas and archipelagos that lie between China and the open Pacific waters. This information is from the unclassified, annual Pentagon-produced report to Congress, "Military and Security Developments Involving the People's Republic of China" (2018 edition).[19]

Of particular interest in this discussion is the second ring denoting the operating radius of the Chinese DF-26 missile, dubbed the "carrier killer." It can carry nuclear or conventional explosives, has multiple independently guided warheads, and as mentioned earlier in this chapter, over a thousand of these missiles can be produced for the price of *one* U.S. carrier strike group.

Most Americans are not aware of the state of China's military advances, and I would urge those readers who have the time and interest to read the annual report on China's military produced by the Department of Defense. It deserves to be widely read and understood by citizens and lawmakers alike to make realistic assessments of the relative military strengths of the United States and China.

If China spends 70 percent of its military budget in its neighborhood ($120 billion), while the United States spends 25 percent of its military budget in the Pacific (US$206 billion), the practical difference in military budgets for both countries in China's neighborhood is $80 billion instead of $653 billion.

The United States feels its national interests require it to try and be the global hegemon, while China aims to be the local hegemon. These self-imposed limits to China's military objectives reduce the practical impact of the difference between U.S. and Chinese defense outlays.

To further strengthen its military domination of the South China Sea, China claims nearly all of the South China Sea by its so-called nine-dash line that is imprinted on Chinese maps of the region, a line that China says encompasses an area that it claims has belonged to China throughout recorded history. Never mind that the Chinese ownership claims are contested by a number of countries surrounding the South China Sea. (Japan has a similar ownership dispute over the Senkaku Islands, called the Diaoyu Islands by China, in the East China Sea.)

To understand why China's claims to the islands, rocks, and shoals of the South China Sea are important to Chinese military domination of the South China Sea (beyond just the raw materials and energy resources that lie on the seabed), it's worth briefly discussing the United Nations Convention on the Law of the Sea (UNCLOS), also called the Law of the Sea treaty.

The Law of the Sea defines the rights and responsibilities of nations with respect to their use of the world's oceans, establishing guidelines for businesses, the environment, and the management of marine natural resources. The treaty was laboriously worked out under the auspices of the United Nations.

Without getting mired in detail, UNCLOS, which took nine years to finalize, states that countries' ownership rights over the waters adjacent to their shoreline extend to 12 nautical miles from their shores. These waters are the country's *territorial waters*. For another 12 nautical miles from territorial waters, an area that is termed the *contiguous zone,* countries can enforce their laws in only four specific areas: customs, taxation, immigration, and pollution. Finally, for 200 nautical miles from shore, the treaty defines an *exclusive economic zone* in which countries have the sole rights to exploit natural resources that lie under the oceans but cannot claim ownership of the sea.

Most of the world, including China, have ratified UNCLOS. The United States has refused to ratify this important treaty even after the U.S. defense and intelligence establishments strongly recommended that the United States do so. The position of the United States Senate vis-à-vis UNCLOS is that although America will not ratify UNCLOS, it will abide by its conventions. The refusal to ratify has to do with a strong feeling in the Senate that the United States should never become a part of anything that impinges on its sovereignty, and UNCLOS (like the International Criminal Court in the Hague) for some Americans falls into this category.

The Law of the Sea clarifies why it is important for China to own most of the South China Sea, including its shoals, islands, reefs, and even large rock formations. For one thing, if it owns all the land features within the South China Sea, by virtue of UNCLOS, it has sole rights to exploit the natural resources that lie under waters that are up to 200 nautical miles from *each* land feature!

Furthermore, as China points out, ownership gives it the right, and indeed the responsibility, to protect its territory by any means necessary. To fulfill its responsibility, China has constructed military facilities, including runways and antiaircraft and antiship batteries on several islands within the South China Sea to extend the range of its defensive weapons and make its military strategies even more effective.

At the beginning of this chapter, I noted that China's Malacca Dilemma has two facets: dominance of the South China Sea and the reduction of

China's reliance on the Strait of Malacca. Besides the substantial commercial reasons that justify the Belt and Road Initiative, several BRI projects are designed to reduce China's reliance on the Strait of Malacca. In fact, numerous Asian geopolitical experts and bankers have told me that, in their opinion, finding ways to address China's Malacca Dilemma is a key reason for the existence of the BRI, and that China would be willing to ensure the success of the BRI projects that help it bypass the Strait of Malacca even if it loses money on them in the short term. The next chapter will explore the projects that illuminate the nexus between BRI's commercial and geopolitical values to China.

FOUR

The Belt and Road Initiative
in Action

"We also know there are known unknowns. That is to say, we know there are some things we do not know. But there are also unknown unknowns—the ones we don't know we don't know . . ."
—Donald Rumsfeld, former U.S. Defense Secretary

Since President Xi Jinping launched the Belt and Road Initiative in 2013, China has launched over 150 projects in Eurasia and Africa under its banner. The known projects are listed in the Appendix. I say "known projects" because there appears to be no official Chinese list of BRI projects. The compilation in the Appendix was drawn from the Reconnecting Asia[1] project of the Center for Strategic and International Studies (CSIS),[2] the best and most authoritative source for Asian infrastructure projects, whether or not BRI funded.

These four projects—the China-Pakistan Economic Corridor (CPEC), the China-Myanmar Economic Corridor, the Sri Lankan port of Hambantota, and China's purchase of the controlling interest in the Greek Port of Piraeus—illuminate both the strategic mindset of China and how much it has yet to learn as the Belt and Road Initiative reaches out into lands far away from China.

In an earlier chapter, I compared the announcement of China's Belt and Road Initiative to the announcement of the American objective of landing a man on the moon. I mentioned then that these were bold, visionary goals that would need to succeed despite the many unknown unknowns—meaning difficulties and problems that would be encountered only during execution. That is what happened on the way to America's moon landing and that is what is happening to China's grand strategy as, to use an American idiom, the rubber hits the road.

American news media and the Trump administration have increasingly begun presenting BRI as a "debt trap" designed by China to lend far more money to unsuspecting countries than the countries should prudently borrow. This might be true on the margins, but the idea of poor, innocent, unsuspecting countries on the one side, and China as a loan shark on the other, is overdone and in most cases factually incorrect.

CHINA-PAKISTAN ECONOMIC CORRIDOR (CPEC)

The China-Pakistan Economic Corridor is the Belt and Road Initiative's marquee project, both for being the largest BRI investment by China in one country (up to US$65 billion)[3] and for the scope and diversity of the planned infrastructure enhancements in one country. These include roads, railways, dams, power-generating stations, airports, schools, hospitals, and the transformation of the Pakistan's Arabian Sea port of Gwadar into a major Indian Ocean maritime hub.[4]

The CPEC is a massive bilateral project to improve infrastructure within Pakistan and between it and China, to enhance trade with China and to further integrate the countries of the region. Add the CPEC projects together and they are geared to make measurable improvements to the economy and quality of life of the people in Pakistan. The 15-year project was launched on April 20, 2015, when President Xi Jinping of China and Prime Minister Nawaz Sharif of Pakistan signed 51 agreements and memoranda of understanding valued at $46 billion. The goal of CPEC is to transform Pakistan's economy—by modernizing its road, rail, air, and energy transportation systems—and to connect the deep-sea Pakistani port of Gwadar to China's Xinjiang Province and beyond by overland routes. (Xinjiang borders the countries of Mongolia, Russia, Kazakhstan, Kyrgyzstan, Tajikistan, Afghanistan, Pakistan, and India.) The China-Pakistan Economic Corridor will reduce the time, cost, and risk of transporting goods and energy such as natural gas to China by circumventing the Straits of Malacca and the South China Sea.[5]

As the consulting firm of Deloitte has pointed out, the value of the CPEC-related projects will exceed *all* foreign direct investment in Pakistan since 1970 and would be equivalent to 17 percent of Pakistan's 2015 gross domestic product. Deloitte estimates that CPEC will generate approximately 700,000 direct jobs over the project's 15-year life cycle and add up to 2.5 percent to Pakistan's growth rate.[6]

The China-Pakistan Economic Corridor's implementation was planned in four stages:

1. 2015–2019: Early harvest projects mostly related to the energy sector. These are already completed or will be by 2019, adding around 10,000 megawatts to the national grid. This has already started to ease the energy shortages that have crippled industry and exports.

2. 2019–2022: Short-term projects are mainly roads, the port of Gwadar development, fiber-optic network, coal mining, and power projects.

3. 2022–2025: Medium-term projects such as railways and industrial zones.

4. 2025–2030: Long-term projects such as completion of industrial zones, agriculture, tourism, and so on.

Prime Minister Nawaz Sharif's government was defeated at the polls in July 2018. Although Sharif's tenure saw the completion of most of the early harvest projects, the incoming government of Prime Minister Imran Khan is reviewing the scope of the CPEC as well as other financial loans and commitments to prepare the country to approach the International Monetary Fund for assistance.

CPEC—BETWEEN THE LINES

Although CPEC is China's marquee project for the Belt and Road Initiative, it has also become the poster child for the West and BRI skeptics to illustrate that the BRI is a scheme put together by China to practice modern-day colonialism.

In this view, the Belt and Road Initiative is a vehicle for China to take advantage of infrastructure-needy (and by implication, naive) countries by saddling them with more debt than they can afford to repay and then exchanging debt for equity—by forcing the indebted countries to turn over ownership of the infrastructure projects to China on long-term leases. In this narrative, China lends more money to countries than they can afford to borrow for their BRI projects. And when these unsuspecting but infrastructure-hungry countries predictably are unable to meet their payment obligations, China plays hardball and takes possession of a project's assets on long-term leases. In the nineteenth century, France and Britain, then the world's leading colonial powers, used this practice, for instance, to underwrite the Suez Canal's construction and then take ownership from the Egyptian government.

These skeptics point out that Pakistan already suffers from a chronic debt problem that can only worsen with the $65 billion that CPEC will ultimately require, much of which Chinese lenders will borrow.

Although this argument may have some justification in other BRI countries, after my conversation about the pros and cons of CPEC with Dr. Ishrat Husain, former governor of the State Bank of Pakistan (the country's central bank), I am convinced that it is factually inaccurate with regard to Pakistan.

For one thing, even though the China-Pakistan Economic Corridor could *ultimately* be a recipient of $67 billion in Chinese financial assistance and loans, as of September 2018, the projects agreed to by the governments of Pakistan and China totaled $45 billion, not $67 billion.

"All other numbers are either speculative or imaginary," Dr. Husain told me. The practical import of Dr. Husain's statement is that calculations of Pakistan's CPEC liabilities should be based on $45 billion, not $67 billion, an important distinction for the calculation of the country's debt burden.

Therefore, using the $45 billion number, over a period of 15 years (the projected life cycle of CPEC), the investment by China will amount to $3 billion a year, which is approximately only 6 percent of the annual investment budget of Pakistan.[7] This percentage, Dr. Husain says, should be equally illuminating to those who exaggerate the impact of CPEC on Pakistan's economy, and those who label CPEC a debt trap for Pakistan.[8]

Further, Dr. Husain told me, CPEC's first phase is front-loaded with power-generation and energy-related projects, or "early harvest" projects, as they are called in CPEC. Most of these are either completed or (as of September 2018) are within a year of completion. The completed projects have already added 10,000 megawatts of electricity-generation capacity to Pakistan's power grid, providing badly needed relief to Pakistan's export companies.

Dr. Husain notes that Pakistan's exports had tumbled from $25 billion to $21 billion because of power shortages that had cost the economy about 1.5 to 2 percentage points of GDP. With the increase in power generation already realized from CPEC projects, exports are growing by double digits.[9]

Husain has analyzed the CPEC loans from China to Pakistan, and his conclusion is that the total annual outflow of cash from Pakistan to China for the repayment of CPEC project loans of $65 billion would average between $2.5 billion to $3 billion dollars. "How would this amount be repaid?" he rhetorically asks. His answer, "As these [power] shortages are eased and efficiency gains are realized, the national income would rise at least by $6–7 billion per annum." More than enough to service the Chinese loans and have enough for new investments.[10] This is a conclusion underscored by the analysis of the International Institute for Applied Systems Analysis, which showed that "A single 1GW electric power plant enables $32 billion of GDP in developing nations."[11]

What I found particularly striking in my conversation with Dr. Husain were his conservative views regarding the gains to Pakistan's economy from the energy projects built into the China-Pakistan Economic Corridor. Although Dr. Husain is convinced that the additional power that has already come online in Pakistan, thanks to CPEC, has the *potential* to yield solid improvements in Pakistan's long-term prospects and raise the standard of living for the average Pakistani citizen, as well as the business community, whether all the gains will actually be realized, he cautions, is not dependent on CPEC's energy infrastructure projects alone, but is in the end a function of the government of Pakistan's internal policies.

For instance, the power sector in Pakistan has perennially had two major issues: a deficit of power availability and an endemic problem of collecting payments, from electricity producers, to power distribution companies, to individual and business consumers. As this book goes to press, CPEC has largely resolved the power generation deficit by adding some 10,000 megawatts to Pakistan's power grid, but the second half of the problem, distribution and payment collection, is yet to be addressed. "A tangle of debts among state generators, energy suppliers and banks has been exacerbated by theft from the grid. This can be resolved by reducing subsidies, raising energy taxes and recapitalizing state entities," notes *The Economist*.[12] This is a benchmark by which to judge Mr. Imran Khan, the new prime minister of Pakistan, and his administration.

Unquestionably, Pakistan's economy is in trouble with its public-debt/GDP ratio of 40 percent, and the country is already seeking financial aid from China, Saudi Arabia, and the IMF. What is clear to me, however, is that the Belt and Road Initiative is not a material cause of Pakistan's debt problems. If anything, the CPEC, with the favorable early results from its energy generation projects, is already part of the solution. Now Prime Minister Khan's government needs the tenacity to legislate changes to Pakistan's subsidy and transmission regimes.

CPEC AND THE MALACCA DILEMMA

It is not for nothing that China's largest BRI project, the China-Pakistan Economic Corridor, is named for what will be the project's most significant outcome: the 1,678 miles (2,700 kilometers) of road and rail links to connect landlocked western China's Xinjiang Province to Pakistan's Arabian Sea port of Gwadar. This will provide China with a deepwater port and a maritime outlet that reduces the need to use the Strait of Malacca. The land connection of highways, railways, and pipelines will bypass the Strait of Malacca and reduce the route for oil deliveries from the Middle East to China from 8,016 miles (12,900 kilometers) to 1,864 miles (3,000 kilometers). CPEC funding has already started to transform Gwadar, which used to be a sleepy fishing village in Pakistan, into a major Indian Ocean maritime transit hub.

It does not take long to appreciate the strategic importance of Gwadar, located as it is at the nexus of central Asia, the Middle East, and Africa, and athwart the sea lanes that connect the Strait of Hormuz to the Indian Ocean. Fully one-fifth of the world's petroleum passes daily through this strait, which makes it a critically important oil artery for transporting oil to China and East Asia. At its narrowest point (off Iran), the strait is barely 29 miles (46.7 kilometers) wide, making it one of the most important naval choke points in the world.[13]

Should China ever strike a deal with Pakistan to also use Gwadar as a naval base for the People's Liberation Army Navy (PLAN), it would put China's military power on the pulse of the world's most important sea routes. And who is to say this might not happen? After all, the port has been leased to China for 43 years, and China is now Pakistan's primary armorer. Gwadar also allows China and Pakistan to monitor the traffic to and from the naval ports of Pakistan's arch competitor, India.

CPEC—GEOPOLITICS

For all the potential benefits of CPEC, with its execution, China has been forced to face up to a long-standing Pakistani internal political issue. Gwadar is at the southern tip of Pakistan's Balochistan Province, which is sparsely populated but richly endowed with natural resources. "The contrast between territory and population largely shapes Balochistan's particular situation and problems. Balochistan's huge territory is home to the greater part of Pakistan's mineral and energy resources . . . [but] its tiny population means that it has little say in Pakistani national politics and little control over how its huge resources are developed," writes Anatol Lieven in his excellent book on Pakistan.[14]

These accusations are part of the reason the Baloch wanted Balochistan to be an independent country but were forced to join Pakistan when colonial India was split up in 1947 by Britain, the area's then colonial power, into a predominantly Hindu India and a predominantly Muslim Pakistan. As Lieven puts it, "[the Baloch] have been dealt a rather poor hand by modern history, and that they have not generally been treated with vision or generosity by Pakistani governments."[15] These lingering enmities have fostered an ongoing armed resistance movement to Pakistan's governance of the province, that has increasingly targeted Chinese workers on CPEC assignments, as reported in this August 2018 incident in the *Nikkei Asian Review*.[16]

> Terrorist attacks on Chinese workers in southwest Pakistan are unnerving Beijing. . . . A suicide bomber wounded six people, including three Chinese engineers, earlier this month in an attack on a bus near the town of Daband in in Balochistan Province. The Baloch Liberation Army, a banned separatist group, claimed responsibility for the blast, saying it was carried out "to warn China to vacate Balochistan and stop plundering its resources." Baloch insurgent groups carried out fatal attacks on Chinese in 2004 and 2006, and earlier this year an unidentified gunman killed the Chinese general manager of COSCO Shipping Lines Company in Karachi. . . . Last week's attack was the first suicide bombing targeting Chinese in Balochistan, which is at the heart of the $62 billion China-Pakistan Economic Corridor. . . ."

The economic benefits that will accrue to Pakistan through the transformation of the village of Gwadar into a major port with the addition of infrastructure to connect the port to Pakistan's rail and road system, and to provide housing, medical facilities, tax-free economic zones, should help resolve this important domestic national security issue that has continued to threaten the internal security of Pakistan.

According to the China-Pakistan Economic Corridor chairman of the Gwadar Port Authority (GPA), Dostain Khan Jamaldini, "The development of Gwadar port will directly benefit Balochistan province and the whole

Pakistan," adding that, "Gwadar is a city of some 110,000 people and such massive industrialisation under the CPEC will have a great impact not only on the city but also on the whole Balochistan province, . . . the Gwadar Free Zone will have the capacity to generate at least 38,000 direct jobs in the remote city."[17]

BENEFITING CHINA'S WESTERN PROVINCES

Besides the land connection from Gwadar to Kashgar in China, the China-Pakistan Economic Corridor also includes oil and gas pipelines, providing yet another alternative not just to transport oil to China, but more specifically, to the western provinces of China, which are some 2,174 miles (3,500 kilometers) from China's east coast ports of Tianjin, Shanghai, and Hong Kong, the main entry points for China's energy supplies.

On the China side of the ledger, CPEC's connection of the western Chinese province of Xinjiang to the sea will materially help the economy of Xinjiang and begin to help China deal with a serious internal issue that is a consequence of its rapid export-driven economic growth—the widening income gap. Xinjiang is among the poorest of China's provinces.

In China's western provinces (of which Xinjiang is one) the average income per capita is half of what it is in the coastal provinces where China's major ports are situated. For instance, in 2016 in Shanghai, income per capita was almost four times as much as it was in Gansu (adjacent to Xinjiang) in northwestern China.[18]

Xinjiang is also home to the Uighurs, China's Turkic-Muslim community, a sizeable minority in China that is already restive because of the Chinese government's plans to place over a million Uighurs in internment camps to "reeducate" them. And finally, Xinjiang is rich in natural resources, especially oil, natural gas, and coal. For all these reasons CPEC's connection of western China to the sea will spark the development of manufacturing facilities, export industries, rail connections, warehouses, and mining, adding materially to Xinjiang's economy.

CPEC—BALANCING THE UNITED STATES AND CHINA

One can also view the China-Pakistan Economic Corridor as a strategic chessboard on which Pakistan is trying to balance its U.S.-China relationships against a mounting pile of foreign direct investment from China. This may prove an impossible task given that China has already replaced the United States as the premier supplier to Pakistan's military, and China's investment in Pakistan through CPEC dwarfs America's.[19]

However, despite the potentially transformational nature of the China-Pakistan Economic Corridor, Pakistan seems eager not to cut its U.S. ties—just yet.

Some 700 kilometers east of Gwadar lies Karachi, Pakistan's biggest and busiest port. It is the starting point for the vast amount of supplies that must be delivered to feed the American war in Afghanistan. In fact, it would not be an exaggeration to say that were it not for Pakistan's permission to use the port of Karachi and Pakistani roads north, the United States would find it prohibitively expensive and logistically impractical to conduct its war in Afghanistan.

Without access to Karachi, the United States would have to fly in supplies from the north of Afghanistan, an alternative that would not just cost many times more than the existing land route, but would require permission to overfly Iran, China, and the Russian-influenced central Asian countries of Turkmenistan, Tajikistan, Kyrgyzstan, Azerbaijan, and Uzbekistan, a highly unlikely prospect.

What is intriguing to think about is that despite the Trump administration's cutoff of financial and military aid to Pakistan, the roads from Karachi to Afghanistan are still open to the United States to transport supplies to wage war, and likely to remain so according to U.S. Defense Secretary Jim Mattis. "No, I'm not concerned about them [Pakistan]," Mattis recently said, speaking to the ground and air lines of communication through Pakistan.[20] Even more bizarre, given the huge Chinese presence in Pakistan through CPEC, the North Atlantic Treaty Organization (NATO) has recently discussed with Pakistan the use of Gwadar to supply Western troops fighting in Afghanistan, a much shorter route that would get supplies to U.S. troops in under 24 hours versus the weeklong transit from Karachi. According to Pakistan's federal minister for weeklong maritime affairs, Hasil Bizenjo, "NATO people told us it would be extremely convenient for them in terms of quick transportation of supplies from Gwadar directly to Kandahar. They are very interested and we are working on it."[21] This raises the surreal possibility of U.S. war-fighting supplies heading to Afghanistan after being unloaded at Gwadar, the Chinese-built port in Pakistan, on sleek new highways built by China, using the fiber-optic connections supplied by China, all this while both China and Pakistan are under U.S. sanctions!

On a final note, much was made of Pakistan's recent change in government and forecasts of incoming Prime Minister Imran Khan's impending review and potential downsizing or outright cancellation of parts of CPEC projects. Instead, in a meeting between Prime Minister Khan and his Chinese counterpart, Li Keqiang, in November 2018, China and Pakistan signed 15 new agreements to strengthen their commercial and economic relationship.[22]

Although, doubtless, CPEC plans will be reviewed and tailored to the new politics in Pakistan, reports of the demise of CPEC are greatly exaggerated.

CHINA-MYANMAR ECONOMIC CORRIDOR (CMEC)

Myanmar occupies a unique geographical position in the BRI, lying at the junction of South Asia and Southeast Asia, and between the Indian Ocean and southwestern China's landlocked Yunnan Province. China is Myanmar's top investment partner and has invested $20 billion in the country between 1988 and May 2018.[23]

On July 6, 2018, Myanmar signed a memorandum of understanding with China agreeing to establish the China-Myanmar Economic Corridor (CMEC), as part of Beijing's Belt and Road Initiative. The estimated 1,056-mile (1,700-kilometer)-long corridor will connect Kunming, the capital of China's Yunnan Province, to Myanmar's major economic checkpoints—first to Mandalay in central Myanmar, then east to Yangon, and west to the Kyaukpyu Special Economic Zone (SEZ).[24]

As part of this project, oil and natural gas pipelines will run from the Bay of Bengal to China. The oil pipeline diversifies the delivery of China's crude oil import routes from the Middle East and Africa, avoiding traffic through the Strait of Malacca. The gas pipeline will allow delivery of natural gas from Myanmar's offshore fields to China.[25]

The China-Myanmar Economic Corridor will reduce Beijing's trade and energy reliance on the Strait of Malacca, become a major factor in lifting the economies of landlocked southwest China, and will connect the Chinese province of Yunnan with three important economic centers in Myanmar as it winds its way from Yunnan to Mandalay in central Myanmar to Yangon, before terminating at the Kyaukpyu Special Economic Zone.[26]

As part of the negotiations between the two countries, Beijing agreed to a deal with the chairman of the Kyaukpyu Special Economic Zone, vowing that the project will not lead to an excessive debt burden on the Myanmar government. Kyaukpyu is a key strategic project under the BRI, as it is expected to boost development in China's landlocked Yunnan Province.

The project will provide China with direct access to the Indian Ocean and allow China's oil imports to bypass the Strait of Malacca. For Myanmar, the CMEC will bring Chinese investment and technical know-how for a wide range of economic sectors, including construction, manufacturing, agriculture, transport, finance, human resources development, telecommunications, and technology.[27]

The Chinese investment comes just in time for two other reasons: Myanmar's economy has been growing very slowly because of the lack of investment. More importantly, there is increasing global discussion of sanctions against Myanmar over the Rohingya issue—the forced expulsion of almost a million of Myanmar's Muslim population to Bangladesh. So more than ever, the country needs China.[28]

The China-Myanmar Economic Corridor at once illustrates both the benefits and challenges of BRI infrastructure developments to China and the host country, as well as China's steep learning curve as it continues work to broaden and deepen its involvement within a culturally, ethnically, and politically diverse collection of 70 countries.

The Malacca Dilemma, great power politics, Chinese insensitivities to local concerns, and the opportunity by the host country, Myanmar, to play off East against West, are all part of the backdrop to this project.

FEEL THE PEBBLES AS YOU CROSS THE STREAM!

Given that 80 percent of China's oil is transported through the Strait of Malacca, new pipelines in Myanmar make a significant contribution to China's continuing quest to reduce its oil dependence on this narrow waterway. The *Financial Times* succinctly summarized this advantage to China, *"The new oil pipeline, which will transport oil shipped from the Middle East, will reduce China's dependency on Malacca by a third* [my emphasis]. The gas pipeline has an annual capacity of 12bn cubic metres, 28 per cent of China's current gas imports."[29]

In this 2013 article, the *Financial Times* reported that the gas pipeline would begin operating in May of that year and the oil pipeline would soon follow. The gas pipeline did begin to pump gas from Myanmar's Shwe gas field in the Bay of Bengal to China as scheduled, but the oil pipeline would not begin operations until 2017, a victim of domestic politics in Myanmar and China.

Several BRI projects in Myanmar had been suspended because of what the local population viewed as China's domineering and insensitive attitude toward them and China's cavalier attitude to the environmental impact of the infrastructure projects on Myanmar's ecology. There were also accusations that the government of Myanmar condoned rude and superior behavior by the Chinese workers imported to work on the projects, to the detriment of the local citizens. In 2014, for instance, more than 20 Burmese workers were detained at a pipeline worksite after a clash with Chinese coworkers, but no Chinese were arrested.

Reporting on the incident, senior reporter Khin OO Tha of *The Irrawaddy* said that "Burmese and Chinese workers living in the same house fought after Chinese workers poured water from an upstairs window and got their Burmese colleagues wet. Other reports have said the Burmese workers believed the Chinese had urinated on them. . . . [A] resident also expressed her opinion that it was not fair to detain Burmese alone for investigation."[30]

These delayed projects included the giant $3.6 billion Myitsone Dam project, one of China's showpiece BRI investments in Myanmar that was designed to generate 6 gigawatts of electricity, but 90 percent of the power was destined for Yunnan Province in China. And thousands of local residents would have to be resettled to build the dam, which would also result in ecological and environmental damage. Not surprisingly, the package generated an avalanche of anti-Chinese sentiment as it dawned on the Burmese that the Myitsone Dam project would mostly benefit China and leave the ecological and environmental detritus in Myanmar. Far from the win-win promised by President Xi Jinping, this project seemed to be offering its riches to China while leaving scraps for the citizens of Myanmar, who would also be left with large debts to pay off in the future.

Besides resettlement, the Burmese object to perceived differing compensation rates paid by the Chinese state-owned company, China Power Investment, responsible for the dam's construction, which would operate the dam for 50 years before transferring it to Myanmar. "When they invest, the Chinese bring their own labor and they discriminate," an aggrieved Burmese told the *East Asia Forum*.[31] "They pay RMB100 ($14.62) for Chinese labour, while they give 35 kyat ($0.03) to local labor. There is no benefit for us to stay together with China. They take away all our resources." As this book goes to press, the Myitsone Dam and hydroelectric project remain suspended pending further negotiations.

The BRI's image in Myanmar was also about to suffer another blow: a last-minute hold pending review by the Myanmar government of another big-ticket, strategically important project—the planned Chinese investment of $7.3 billion to construct a deepwater port and a special economic zone (SEZ) at Kyaukpyu on the Bay of Bengal, at the terminal point of the Kyauk-pyu to Kunming oil and gas pipelines.

The backdrop to this suspension of a high-visibility project was the BRI-developed port of Hambantota in Sri Lanka. As we shall shortly see, the Sri Lankan government was unable to repay China's loans to develop Ham-bantota, and with China's hardball, bill-collector tactics, was forced to turn the port over to Chinese control for a 99-year lease.

In a humbling turnaround, under pressure from Myanmar, the $7.3 bil-lion investment, that could have climbed to $10 billion if the China-proposed SEZ and 4,200-acre industrial park to attract textile and oil refining indus-tries had proceeded, was dramatically scaled down to around $1.3 billion, and the original plans to develop 10 berths to handle large oil tankers was reduced to two berths.[32] In an effort to contain the public relations fallout from this BRI setback, China portrayed the scale-down as only the first phase of a four-phase project. As the *Independent* reported, "China's state-run CITIC Group, the main developer of the project, said negotiations were ongoing and that the $1.3bn was to be spent on the 'initial phase' of the port, adding the project was divided into four phases. It did not elaborate on plans for subsequent stages."[33]

GEOPOLITICS

The geopolitical complexity of this turn of events impacted both China and Myanmar. For China, it vividly demonstrated the scrutiny that its BRI project proposals will face going forward, and the dangers to its carefully cultivated image of BRI's magnanimous image. The heyday of proposals being accepted by host countries at face value, without rigorous financial analysis, simply as a goodwill gesture by China, appear to be over.

But in the Kyaukpyu project, Myanmar also faces a dilemma. Kyauk-pyu lies at the southern end of Myanmar's Rakhine State where almost a million Rohingya Muslims have fled Myanmar for neighboring Bangladesh to avoid purportedly wholesale slaughter by Myanmar's armed forces. These actions have resulted in Western sanctions and the portrayal of Myanmar as an inhumane military-led regime. This made it essential for Myanmar to retain China's diplomatic support.

As the United States could unhappily testify, the road to global promi-nence is strewn with potholes!

But then, as India's daily, *The Hindu,* reported on September 15, 2018, "China's Belt and Road Initiative (BRI) got a high octane boost last week, when Myanmar—facing the heat from the West because of the Rohingya refugee crisis—inked an agreement with Beijing to establish a cross border economic corridor."

Insensitivity to Myanmar's domestic politics and environment almost cost China a large part of this project, an important part of China's plan to cut down its reliance on the Strait of Malacca. As China and the BRI were about to get a bloody nose for their insensitivity to the host country, the West stepped in and saved the day for China by a virulent stream of criticism directed at Myanmar's State Counsellor (equivalent to prime minister) Aung San Suu Kyi and her generals for their callous and inhumane treatment of hundreds of thousands of Rohingya Muslims who were forced to flee for their lives into the neighboring country of Bangladesh.

As justified as the Western criticism might have been, it sent a message to Myanmar's leader, Ms. Suu Kyi, that she had better strike a compromise with China if she wanted to improve her country's economy because Myanmar was not going to get a deal at all from the West.

A decade ago, Myanmar would not have had an option but to give in to the West's criticism and meekly take what aid it got, but now it had a powerful alternative—China's Belt and Road Initiative. What had been designed as a nameless project with 497 miles (800 kilometers) of oil and gas pipelines was transformed into a 1,056-mile (1,700-kilometer) project that included several other infrastructure enhancements with a shiny new name—the China-Myanmar Economic Corridor. Chalk up another strategically important country on China's side. A delighted Myanmar's State Counsellor Aung San Suu Kyi's administration now gets capital and technology to develop the country, thus consolidating power that has been challenged by the opposition.

My point here is not, and I emphasize *not,* to criticize the West's critique of the horrendous treatment of the Rohingyas, who were subjected to rape, torture, and murder ostensibly by Myanmar government troops, or at the least with the troops turning a blind eye to the atrocities. Rohingya homes were set on fire, and they were driven from their ancestral homes into a neighboring impoverished country, Bangladesh. My point simply is that the BRI gave Myanmar an option. Myanmar had considered the West's criticism to be overdone and unrealistic given local politics and sensitivities, but it needed the investment into its economy. So, State Counsellor Aung San Suu Kyi struck a compromise with China, adjusted some of the projects that China had originally proposed to better suit Myanmar' politics and economics, and inked a new deal under BRI auspices. Without the Belt and Road Initiative, Myanmar would have had to adjust its internal policy to Western idealism to get the funds it needed. The BRI gave it a powerful alternative, which it took.

SRI LANKA AND THE PORT OF HAMBANTOTA

The basics of the Hambantota story are easy to understand. In 2010, Sri Lanka's then government negotiated a deal with China to develop the country's second major port in the town of Hambantota. The port of Hambantota lies at the southern tip of Sri Lanka and is strategically important because it is located only 60 miles (97 kilometers) from major maritime sea routes from the Middle East and Africa to the Strait of Malacca and on to China.

The port of Hambantota also lies midway between major Middle Eastern ports such as Dubai and Singapore. If Hambantota were to be developed into a major port with container handling, bunkering, warehousing, and transshipment facilities, it could offer shipping companies a convenient stopping point in the Indian Ocean between the Middle East and Singapore.

Most importantly, Hambantota is a key port of naval importance in China's so-called "string of pearls" strategy, the network of Chinese ports and relationships along its maritime routes. These extend from the Chinese mainland to Port Sudan, of which Sri Lanka is a key "pearl." Without Hambantota, the entire east coast of India would be outside one strand of the "pearls." The Maldives "pearl," is not yet finalized due to strong Indian objections, so without Hambantota, China's "string of pearls" strategy would have a big missing link from Bangladesh to the Pakistani port of Gwadar—a part of the Indian Ocean that contains some of the most important maritime routes in the world.

It also goes without saying that Hambantota's location athwart major maritime shipping lanes gives it military and strategic importance, both of which would make a good case for the investment to develop it into a major port. Which is what then president of Sri Lanka, Mr. Mahinda Rajapaksa, was determined to do. The town of Hambantota where the port would be located had one other advantage, which cannot be measured on a financial balance sheet. It lies in the constituency represented by the president! Is there a politician anywhere in the world who would not want to support a project that benefits the people in his or her constituency?

Ultimately, Sri Lanka borrowed $1.3 billion from China and poured most of it into the development of Hambantota's port, which opened for business in 2010, but has found it hard to make money and continues to incur losses. With these continuing losses, the Sri Lankan government found it impossible to make the loan payments and went into arrears. At this point, President Rajapaksa was defeated in a general election by Ranil Wickremesinghe. The incoming prime minister took one look at Sri Lanka's empty treasury and realized that he had no choice but to renegotiate the loan terms for the Hambantota Port project.

In December 2017, Sri Lanka turned over 80 percent of the port, together with 15,000 acres around the port, under a 99-year lease to China Merchants Port Holdings, a Chinese government entity that operates several Asian ports. The debt for equity deal erased $1 billion of Chinese debt from Sri Lanka's balance sheet.[34]

As part of the deal, China Merchants Port Holdings agreed to make a further $1.7 billion investment in Hambantota, add an economic zone and an industrial park to its facilities, and make it into one of the Indian Ocean's most attractive ports. In addition, the agreement requires the Chinese firm to pay an annual fee to Sri Lanka.

That is essentially the history of the Hambantota project. I suspect any junior investment banker would applaud the difficult decision the Sri Lankan government made to reduce its indebtedness and set itself on the road to solvency, but that is not the way the media and BRI critics see it.

GEOPOLITICS

If the China-Pakistan Economic Corridor is the marquee project of China's Belt and Road Initiative, the Sri Lankan port of Hambantota is the poster child for Western accusations that the BRI is a means for China to make imprudently large loans to unsuspecting countries. When these countries cannot pay back the loans, China grabs the geopolitical and economically prized assets that were funded by the loans.

The port of Hambantota in Sri Lanka, together with the deepwater port in Kyaukpyu, Myanmar, and the China-Pakistan Economic Corridor have all been widely reported to have fallen into this Chinese loan-sharking racket. A needy but impoverished country gets encouragement from China to get greedy and borrow lots of money to develop infrastructure. Then the country cannot make the loan payments to China, and China becomes an ironfisted debt collector, calls in the loan, and takes over the assets for which the poor, unsuspecting country borrowed money. Onward to the next unsuspecting country to pick up more assets with a smile and offer of BRI money for infrastructure development.

As discussed earlier in this chapter, the accusations of loan-sharking by China in Pakistan are inaccurate at best because these projects never got to the loan-sharking level. In Myanmar, China's insensitive handling of the BRI projects almost got the deals killed, but, as we have seen, negotiations with compromises on both sides have put BRI investment in Myanmar back on track. Hambantota in Sri Lanka comes closest to proving the BRI skeptics' claims. But only just. As is usually the case, reality in Asia concerning the award of large contracts is much more nuanced.

"How China Got Sri Lanka to Cough Up a Port" was the headline of a June 2018 front-page *New York Times* story.[35] Breitbart in turn warned that with the port's sale, China was "undermining the country's sovereignty, and . . . widespread concerns China would use it as a military base."[36]

I simply do not buy it, for at least three reasons.

Government deals of this size rarely take place in Asia (nor, albeit to a lesser extent, elsewhere) without the ruling party benefiting from them in some way. In fact, a *New York Times* article does an excellent job of uncovering how China Merchants Port Holding illegally sluiced at least $7.6 million toward getting Mr. Rajapaksa reelected.[37]

I might point out that India, one of the loudest critics of Hambantota's lease, was itself caught up in a major payback scandal involving then Prime Minister Rajiv Gandhi (together with a number of his party politicians). He was accused of receiving kickbacks from Bofors, the famous Swedish military supplier, in a contract bid to supply artillery to the Indian Army.[38] One needs to keep a realistic attitude to deal making when doing multimillion-dollar deals in Asia, and in fairness might I say, anywhere in the world.

It seems to me that the impoverished, rural, and undeveloped—but full of potential—area that encompasses the port of Hambantota in southern Sri Lanka may ultimately benefit from the development that will now take place with a highly experienced and well-heeled majority owner that can afford to complete and market the project.

Although it is true that few ships call at Hambantota now, it does not have to be that way forever. If, that is, the property is developed and marketed. As the "takeover" lease points out, "Hambantota Port is a comprehensive deep-water port, with 10 . . . specialized berths to handle containers, bulk cargos, . . . and liquid bulk. [With] water depth of 17 meters, (56 feet), which makes Hambantota Port . . . capable of handling super-mega vessels . . . The significant landmass of the project (approximately 11.5 sq. kilometers (11 sq. miles) port area) gives leeway for the Group to implement and capitalize . . . to add substantial value to the port operations and development."

With the new owners contractually pledged to finance these developments with an investment of $1.12 billion,[39] and with the Sri Lanka government's retention of approximately 15 percent ownership of the project, it is time to review the label of Chinese colonialism that has been attached to Hambantota and use a less controversial phrase for China's actions in Sri Lanka—classic Wall Street opportunistic takeover move perhaps?

The innocent-victim theory seemed to be the main premise of the lengthy June 2018 *New York Times* article that I referenced earlier.[40] Might the readers of this column have started off with a different perspective if they had known that Prime Minister Rajapaksa, the person who signed the loan documents that "coughed up the port," was himself a lawyer,[41] who practiced law in a southern Sri Lanka town "which kept him closely in touch with the voters and their needs, and also the development needs of the southern region [where the Belt and Road Initiative project would ultimately be located]."[42] An innocent and, gullible Asian leader indeed!

Although Hambantota does not directly contribute to reducing China's reliance on the Strait of Malacca, it does add to China's security needs by adding another key port and potential naval base in China's "string of pearls" strategy.

Unquestionably, the 99-year lease of the port and surrounding assets has given China a significant geopolitical benefit—ownership of a port that is 10 miles from some of the busiest maritime routes from the Middle East and Africa to Asia and that has the potential to provide China significant intelligence, military, and commercial benefits. But 99 years is a long time, and China's regional geostrategic competitor, India, is not the type to sit by and watch from the sidelines as China builds a commercial and military presence in India's backyard.

For instance, as speculation grew about China's military aspirations at Hambantota Port, Sri Lanka announced on June 2018 that the Sri Lanka Navy was moving its Southern Command to Hambantota. Asked what Sri Lanka would do if Chinese troops land in Hambantota, the prime minister responded that there is a full army division stationed at Hambantota, and that Hambantota Port "will only be a commercial port which will trigger off much needed economic development of Hambantota and Monaragala very soon."[43]

India's response to Sri Lanka's announcement that it would move its Southern Naval Command to Hambantota is also worth noting. Two military officials told the *Hindustan Times* that "Enhanced Sri Lankan naval presence in Hambantota . . . would be a positive for India as it would facilitate regular port calls by vessels from India, the United States, Japan and even Australia . . . [and it] will enable better monitoring of the port than is currently happening. This would have some deterrent effect on Chinese activity and also put greater pressure on Sri Lanka for ensuring non-military use compliance," said one of the military officials.[44]

There is no question in my mind that China, the regional hegemon, could land troops or move naval units into Hambantota by force, were it ever to get involved in a major shooting war in the Indian Ocean. It has that military capability. But absent such a conflict, I do not believe China would want to do so. It has the squeaky-clean image of the Belt and Road Initiative to maintain in 70 countries. And after all, Hambantota Port is not one of the reefs or rock outcroppings in the South China Sea that China has claimed as its territory and militarized. It is prime commercial real estate with a promise of long-term returns on investment. The kind of deals that China prizes. That Hambantota has military potential just makes it that much more desirable.

PORT OF PIRAEUS IN GREECE

In Greek mythology, the Golden Fleece is the fleece of the golden-haired winged ram and is a symbol of authority and kingship. Whether Jason brought back the Golden Fleece to the port of Piraeus in Athens, Greece, millennia ago, may be open to debate. What is not, is that in April 2016, China delivered the modern equivalent of the mythical symbol of authority, wealth, and kingship to Greece, in the form of approximately $9 billion (€8 billion) for the purchase, by the Chinese shipping group COSCO, of a controlling interest in Piraeus. The amount includes $570 million (€500 million) dedicated to building new facilities in the port, an annual fee payable to the Greek state, future investments, and the interest to which Greece will have access later. This money allowed the government of Greece to make a loan payment to its international creditors and stave off bankruptcy.[45]

Sixty percent of China's exports already go through Greece, and with the investments that China is required to make in Piraeus, what had been a middling and outdated port is already on its way to rival Europe's biggest ports, such as Rotterdam, Antwerp, and Hamburg.

A grand design overlays the commercial decision for China's purchase of Piraeus. Piraeus is a vital node of the Belt and Road Initiative's global maritime connection. With Piraeus, trade with the Middle East and Africa can eliminate the journey through the Strait of Malacca to China's eastern ports. Instead, goods can flow through the Suez Canal to the port of Piraeus and then on high-speed rail links (now being built by China to Europe from where regularly scheduled train service built under Belt and Road Initiative projects already connects European cities to China).

With the agreement, China got controlling interest in a historic and strategically placed, but down-at-the-heels, European port that has served as a major maritime hub from Greece to central Europe, North Africa, and Asia for centuries. It is worth noting that Greece and China already had a thriving commercial relationship prior to the Piraeus deal. Greece has the largest fleet of commercial vessels in the world, and 60 percent of China's export goes through the country. In addition to the agreement on Piraeus, Chinese banks provide loans to Greece to enable it to have ships built in China. The two countries also cooperate on maritime research and development programs at their universities, according to Hungary's Pallas Athene Geopolitical Research Institute.[46]

For Greece, the sale of the controlling interest in Piraeus was a breath of fresh air and marked the beginning of a badly needed turnaround for the ailing Greek economy. China's prize was a portal to the European Union and its 500 million people, the largest market in the world.

COMMERCE AND GEOPOLITICS

"After years of struggling under austerity imposed by European partners and a chilly shoulder from the United States, Greece has embraced the advances of China, its most ardent and geopolitically ambitious suitor," wrote the *New York Times* on the occasion. "While the Europeans are acting towards Greece like medieval leeches, the Chinese keep bringing money," said Costas Douzinas, head of the Greek Parliament's Foreign Affairs and Defense Committee and a member of the governing Syriza party."

COSCO, the Chinese state-owned company and the world's fourth largest port operator, had already been operating Piraeus's only container terminal, and will invest $261 million (€230 million) to build a second container terminal. The deal also includes guaranteed Chinese investment in the port for years to come.

"Let the ships sail and bring the Golden Fleece," said COSCO Chairman Xu Lirong, couching the deal through the lens of Jason and the Argonauts, no doubt to also remind Greeks that their two countries also share long histories.[47] "The company will continue to be committed to Greek long-term growth and will invest in upgrading the infrastructure at the port and new jobs would be created," he added.[48]

With Chinese technology and investment, Piraeus is rapidly becoming the Mediterranean's most efficient port and is already China's commercial door into Europe. This role will become even more pronounced when a planned rail link is constructed to connect Piraeus with Budapest, Hungary, a project that will bring Chinese products into the heart of central Europe and serve as a conduit for European Union exports to China. In fact, the port of Piraeus is a vital link in completing the Africa-Eurasia-China infrastructure network envisioned by President Xi Jinping when he unfurled the Belt and Road Initiative.

CHINA'S INROADS INTO THE EUROPEAN UNION

Besides the commercial benefits of the port of Piraeus, China was also preparing to play for higher stakes, to lure cash-starved eastern and central European countries away from their exclusively European Union orbits by challenging the assumption that expanding the Belt and Road Initiative into countries that are European Union members requires China to follow EU rules and regulations.

"China Makes Gains in West's Backyard" was a *Wall Street Journal* front-page headline in November 2018. "Deal by deal," the *Wall Street Journal* said, "applying experience honed in Asia and Africa, China is constructing parallel financial and commercial networks in Central and Eastern Europe. . . . It has taken footholds in more than a dozen nations on the periphery of the European Union. . . . Chinese workers set a highway through Montenegro's impassable mountains on pillars as tall as a 50-floor skyscraper part of an emerging corridor of highways, ports and rail lines that outlines a new Chinese trade route between Greece's Aegean coast and Latvia on the frigid Baltic."[49]

But more surprises were in store for the European Union. Being part of the EU assumes its members share common values and adhere to the geopolitical consensus forged by their European partners. Tow the EU line, so to speak. But with China's entry into the EU's backyard, that sacred assumption may not hold any more.

A first shot across the European Union's bow arrived in 2016, almost as soon as the ink was dry on China's investment and purchase agreement with Greece for the port of Piraeus, in what had been thought to be a routine EU declaration asking China to follow a ruling by an international arbitration panel against China's claim to own virtually all of the South China Sea. To the astonishment of European Union officials, three EU countries (Greece, Hungary, and Croatia) refused to go along with the declaration, which had the powerful support of EU heavyweights Britain, Germany, and France. "Some EU countries don't want to annoy China," an aggravated European diplomat complained. Other diplomats sadly noted that "it would be better to abandon efforts to adopt a common statement, in order to avoid further embarrassment for the EU."[50] But this was just the beginning.

The following year, for the first time ever, the European Union was unable to make its annual statement at the U.N. Human Rights Council in Geneva. Greece had blocked the European Union statement condemning China's human-rights record at the council, sparking criticism from human rights groups. "We are deeply disappointed that . . . Greece was not willing to support an appropriately strong expression of concern at the deteriorating human rights situation in China, a situation that warrants serious attention," stated the American nongovernmental organization Human Rights Watch. The Greek official haughtily replied that, "Unconstructive and selective criticism towards specific countries does not help.[51]

More was yet to come, this time unfolding yet another layer of China's grand strategy in the form of a new Chinese geopolitical initiative—the annual summit of a China-led group of 16 central and eastern European countries called the China-Central and Eastern European Countries (CCEEC) or 16 + 1 Initiative. Of the 16 countries, 11 are EU members, and the remaining 5 aspire to EU membership.

China set up the annual summit in 2012, a few months before formally announcing the Belt and Road Initiative, but the group's annual meeting really came into its own as Chinese investment began to pour into central and eastern Europe. Since 2012, China's investment in the 16 countries has risen by 300 percent from $3 billion to over $9 billion.[52]

As the *New Eastern Outlook* noted, the 6th annual summit of the "16 + 1" hosted in November 2017 by Hungary was barely mentioned in the Western press but was noted with alarm in Europe. The opening keynote speech by Hungary's Prime Minister Victor Orban set a new tone for an EU member. Orban proclaimed that "Europe's most competitive investment environment has come into being in Central and Eastern Europe." Noting that not too long ago, Asia depended on the West for investment in modernization, today, "the star of the East is now in the ascendant," and we live in an era marked by the rise of Asia—and within it, China. "We are at the beginning of a period in which the further development of Europe will be dependent on the technological and financial involvement of the East."[53]

The four Belt and Road Initiative projects discussed in this chapter illustrate China's determined efforts to achieve global prominence, create its own grouping of scores of allied countries, set up a reliable supply of natural resources, and reduce its reliance on the Strait of Malacca, all at the same time. All four projects also illuminate the enormity of the task that lies ahead for China as it executes its grand strategy for global prominence. Not for nothing has the Belt and Road Initiative been dubbed the largest infrastructure project in history!

I quoted then Secretary of Defense Donald Rumsfeld earlier in this chapter. His memorable phrase "unknown unknowns" that the United States faced in its ill-fated invasion of Iraq has become a staple of that war's literature, as it now has, in my opinion, for the execution of China's Belt and Road Initiative. All four projects in this chapter testify to that. The difference is that America did not seem to learn from encountering the "unknown unknowns" in Iraq, but China has, so far, shown an ability to self-correct and make up for its lack of understanding and sensitivities as it reaches out from Beijing to Croatia, Lagos, and beyond.

I need to bring into focus one remaining piece of the Belt and Road Initiative to complete the understanding of this massive project, and that is the BRI and Africa. Unlike in Asia and Europe, China is following a much more complex strategy in Africa. China wants to transform Africa into the next manufacturing giant in the world, even as it connects this huge continent into the BRI. This final piece of China's grand strategy is the subject of the next chapter.

The BRI is too far advanced in its execution and branding to be blocked by the United States (or the European Union) with almost trivial attempts to portray China's grand strategy in terms of "empire, aggression and imperialism" in Asia,[54] a charge belied by the tangible benefits of BRI that are already evident in dozens of Asian, European, and African countries. But there are ways in which the two superpowers of the twenty-first century can yet work together for the benefit of both countries and the world.

FIVE

Africa, the BRI's Meeting Point

"If you want to get rich, build yourself a manufacturing industry."
—Irene Yuan Sun

September is praised as a golden month in Beijing, the *Travel China Guide* tells us. It is cool, clear, and brisk. Everywhere presents a harvest scene. The rainy season and summer heat have gone. September, the popular guide to visiting China points out, is a good time to visit Beijing.[1]

And, so it was on September 3 and 4, 2018, when President Xi Jinping welcomed most of the leaders of Africa's 55 countries (49 of 55 attended, the others, mainly smaller African countries, sent lower-ranking officials instead) to gather in Beijing for the third summit meeting of the Forum on China-Africa Cooperation (FOCAC). In fact, if one had to do business in Africa that week, one was simply out of luck; as *Africa News* put it, the continent was almost bereft of presidents; they were all in China mingling with Xi Jinping, the president of China, and his special guest, the president of the United Nations![2]

FOCAC 2018 was yet another example, if one is needed, of how successful China has been in capturing the hearts and minds of the people of Africa, a continent that comprises the largest remaining prize of consequence—a source of competitive workers and a steadily growing pool of middle-class consumers, fertile ground for new wealth creation, and a fast-growing mass consumer market of the 21st century. The very size of Africa makes its potential a big deal. Africa's land area is larger than that of China, the United States, India, and all of Europe, *combined!* By 2025, according to the U.S. Chamber of Commerce, Africa's household expenditures will total US$2.1 trillion, and the continent will be home to over 2.5 billion people by 2050. Africa is poised to become the largest business opportunity since China embraced capitalism.

Add the commercial and soft power benefits of China's African investments to those that will accrue to it from the Belt and Road Initiative and one begins to understand why China is fast replacing the United States as the dominant commercial player and influencer in this vast African continent.

As if to underscore the geopolitical influence that China now wields in Africa, President Xi Jinping made a special point of welcoming four new members to the 2018 FOCAC summit: Gambia, Sao Tome, Principe, and Burkina Faso, all of whom, in spite of strenuous lobbying by the United States, had cut their ties with Taiwan and set up diplomatic relations with China, leaving eSwatini (formerly Swaziland) as the lone African country that still recognized Taiwan.[3]

Already in 2016, China had doubled its foreign direct investment projects in Africa to a level where the value of these projects outweighed U.S. investments by a factor of 10; China–Africa trade had increased by 16.8 percent year-on-year in the first quarter of 2017; and China's infrastructure projects generated earnings of around US$50 billion a year, creating numerous jobs for Chinese citizens.[4]

To demonstrate how well and for how long China had been planning for the 2018 FOCAC, Grisons Peak, a leading China investment research firm, estimated that China had either made or committed to investing $83 billion over the prior 20 months leading to the conference![5] Here are just a few of the investments that I have selected from Grisons Peak to illuminate the size, diversity, and geographic spread of China's Africa strategy:

- Tunisia—memorandum of understanding for BRI (2018)
- Algeria—satellite launch (April 2018) and funded one of the world's largest mosques
- Senegal became the first West African country to sign a BRI cooperation agreement
- Liberia and China agreed (July 2018) to build an artificial hair processing and export hub in Africa. China had already invested over a billion dollars into Liberia over the past 10 years
- Cote d'Ivoire—launch of $580 million hydro project (November 2017) and $47.3 million in new deals (March 2018)

- Ghana—China pledged $10 billion to develop Ghana's bauxite industry (July 2017)
- Nigeria—disclosure that China had invested $45 billion to date in the Nigerian economy
- South Africa—$14.7 billion pledge, all on specific projects
- Cameroon—Chinese companies and Cameroon Telecom began laying a 6,000-kilometer cable linking Cameroon to Brazil, the first cable to link Africa and Latin America

To compete with China's foreign direct investment, from Chinese entrepreneurs and under the Belt and Road Initiative the United States trotted out its secretary of state, Mike Pompeo, a couple of months before the FOCAC conference to announce America's "Indo-Pacific Economic Vision." Clearly, the United States was not going to let the challenge of BRI go unanswered. America's riposte to China's foray into Asia and Africa had all the impact of a damp squib. "US competes with China's 'Belt and Road Initiative' with US$113 million Asian investment programme," sniffed Shi Jiangtao of Hong Kong's *South China Morning Post* on July 30, 2018. When compared with China's trillion-dollar BRI investment, the Asians were unimpressed!

As impressive as China's BRI plans in Africa are, they are only a part of what makes China's overall Africa strategy so effective. Unlike the Belt and Road Initiative's single-minded focus on infrastructure building in other parts of the world, China has a two-pronged strategy in Africa: to ensure the expansion of BRI itself to tie Africa into China's global infrastructure connectivity plans, but—and this is where China's strategy differs from that in Asia and Europe—a continent-wide strategy for placing China at the center of Africa's transformation into the next factory of the world, and to thereby harness Africa's future growth and consumer demand as the engine to power China's continuing trajectory to global primacy.

China's unprecedented growth was powered by its transformation to the world's largest manufacturing and export-driven economy. Now, as manufacturing costs in China become increasingly uncompetitive, China plans to transform Africa to replace it as the factory of the world. As China helps Africa become the world's manufacturing center, it is simultaneously helping Africa to build the infrastructure to connect African countries to each other and to African ports through which Africans can trade between themselves and export to other world countries, and in time become a huge middle-class consumer-driven market, the very path that China itself followed over the last four decades. It is a plan that will reap rich dividends for the Chinese entrepreneurs who are investing money and time all over Africa to execute this transformation plan.

What has not changed in this tailored-for-Africa strategy is the win-win philosophy that China insists underpins the Belt and Road Initiative. Witness the attendance at the 2018 Forum on China-Africa Cooperation in Beijing of almost every African country leader.

Because of its importance to Africa's, China's, and the world's economy, and the fact that it is not widely known, it is worth taking the time to understand China's Africa-as-the-factory-of-the-world plans, before continuing to follow the BRI's maritime journey as it moves through Africa into Europe and finally connects with the BRI's economic belt that runs overland from China through central Asia and Russia to Europe.

CHINA'S AFRICA-AS-THE-FACTORY-OF-THE-WORLD STRATEGY

What I find particularly intriguing in China's Africa-as-the-factory-of-the-world strategy is that the strategy is the very same one that China used to transform *itself* to the world's powerhouse economy.

As Irene Yuan Sun, colead of McKinsey and Company's work on Chinese economic engagement in Africa and the lead author of McKinsey's research report on this topic, observes in her well-researched book, *The Next Factory of the World: How Chinese Investment Is Reshaping Africa,*[6] China pole-vaulted to the top of the world's economic league by disregarding the mantra preached by Washington-led financial and development organizations, such as the World Bank and the International Monetary Fund, that developing countries should focus on limited government and privatization; China chose instead the policy of government-fueled industrialization executed by entrepreneurs to convert itself into the factory of the world. The results of that contrarian decision speak for themselves.

In the 1980s, when China began to rebuild its economy from the wreck of the cultural revolution and its Great Leap Forward program, China had one-fifth of the world's population but produced only 3 percent of global manufacturing output. It was poorer on a per capita basis than many African countries. Today, China accounts for over a quarter of the world's manufacturing output; its gross domestic product has grown at nearly 10 percent a year for three decades, lifting, as was pointed out earlier, some 750 million people out of poverty, the largest and fastest growth in a country's standard of living in recorded history.[7] Within the next decade, China is expected to overtake the United States as the largest economy in the world.

As Ms. Sun states in her book, "Despite the current hype about the rise of robotics and the possibility of fully automating production, the current factory model, in which real people make tangible goods, is far from dead. *If you want to get rich, build yourself a manufacturing industry*" [emphasis mine], she says. And that is just what the Africans are doing.

"Factories are the bridge that connects China, the current Factory of the World, to Africa, the next Factory of the World,"[8] Ms. Sun tells us in her book. "Industrialization is how China reshaped itself from a poor, backward country into one of the largest economies in the world in less than three decades. By becoming the next Factory of the World, Africa can do the same," she says. And her book provides ample evidence that Africa is well on the way to doing this.

Manufacturing is not just a bridge that connects China to Africa; it is a 16-lane superhighway that, en masse, is moving Chinese manufacturing expertise, entrepreneurs, and its factories to Africa. To explain this development, Ms. Sun introduces readers to the *flying geese theory,* business-school jargon that seeks to explain the rapid industrialization of East Asian countries in the twentieth century. The theory postulates that manufacturing firms act like flying geese, migrating from country to country and from product to product, as costs and demands change, and factories become uncompetitive.

Japan became the first East Asian country to bootstrap itself into one of the world's leading economies by industrializing. Its rise in living standards was then the fastest ever seen. But rising costs of production in Japan forced Japanese firms to relocate abroad, to Hong Kong, Singapore, South Korea, and Taiwan. This in turn triggered a new wave of economic transformation, converting these four rickety economies into rich industrialized countries.[9]

Japanese entrepreneurs spawned a wave of Taiwanese entrepreneurs, who spawned a wave of Chinese ones. The fact that Chinese entrepreneurs are now running factories in Africa gives rise to the possibility that the next wave of entrepreneurs and factory owners may very well be African."[10] Ms. Sun's book provides impeccably researched evidence that this manufacturing wave has been well under way in Africa for decades, under Chinese stewardship.

In the year 2000, Chinese companies made a mere two investments in Africa; today they make hundreds. A recent research project coheaded by Ms. Sun showed that there are already more than 10,000 Chinese firms in Africa. In one African country alone, Nigeria—whose population will be greater than that of the United States by 2050—Chinese carmakers, construction materials producers, and consumer goods manufacturers are busy jockeying to compete for its vast business market. In Lesotho, "Chinese garment factories make yoga pants for Kohl's, jeans for Levi's and athletic wear for Reebok. Almost all of Lesotho's production is trucked out and packed onto container ships bound for American consumers," she tells us.

But what about the oft heard criticism, that Chinese firms do not hire Africans? Ms. Sun's research of a thousand Chinese firms that employ more than 300,000 people showed exactly the opposite: More than 95 percent of the employees in manufacturing were Africans.[11] In fact, most contracts for work done by Chinese firms in Africa now clearly specify the number of African workers to be employed on projects. "It is a myth that no Africans get to work on these projects," says Wenjie Chen, an economist in the African Department of the International Monetary Fund. The Chinese go to Africa because of cheap labor and because labor costs in China itself are rising. "You can read it in the [IMF] staff reports. . . . [T]here is an explicit number of African workers," Chen says.[12]

The Chinese are already heavily invested in creating the next factory of the world in Africa. As this Chinese strategy is executed, and African countries are set on trajectories that will make them wealthy, the Chinese entrepreneurs who are jump-starting the next act in Africa's economic development will themselves continue their path to further riches. Which great power will be left out of this next big economic story? No prizes for guessing it will be the United States that appears to have no strategy for Africa.

THE BELT AND ROAD INITIATIVE IN AFRICA

With that overview of one prong of China's African strategy, I'd like to return to the Belt and Road Initiative and examine the BRI projects along Africa's eastern seaboard—in Kenya, Uganda, Ethiopia, Djibouti, and Egypt—that are the anchor points for the penultimate maritime road portion of the Belt and Road Initiative, from its landfall in Kenya, as it moves through the Red Sea and the Suez Canal into the Mediterranean Sea (see Maps 5.1 and 5.2), and finally terminates at Athens, Greece, at the port of Piraeus. This African leg of BRI, from landfall in Kenya to exit in the Mediterranean Sea, is a vital commercial link that connects trade between Europe, Asia, and Africa. And thanks to the BRI, it is rapidly falling under the influence of China, commercially and militarily.

In doing so, the African leg of the BRI touches the countries of Kenya, Djibouti, and Egypt, and illuminates yet again the close link between the

Map 5.1   Djibouti, China's first naval outpost

Belt and Road Initiative and China's no-holds-barred objective to dominate commercial and strategic links everywhere in the world.

KENYA

The importance of Kenya lies in the fact that its Indian Ocean port of Mombasa is the westernmost point of landfall for the Belt and Road's maritime route. Mombasa is the terminal point for the BRI maritime road after it traverses the long route from ports on the east coast of China, passes through the Strait of Malacca, and traverses the Indian Ocean.

KENYA STANDARD GAUGE RAILWAY PROJECT (SGR)

Under a $3.8 billion BRI project, China has financed and built Africa's first electrified railway. It connects Kenya's main port of Mombasa to its capital Nairobi. Construction of the 378-mile (609-kilometer) rail line began in 2013, and was completed on schedule in 2017. The railway line is aimed at easing transport of passengers and cargo between Mombasa and Nairobi. In its future phases, the Mombasa-to-Nairobi railway will connect Kenya

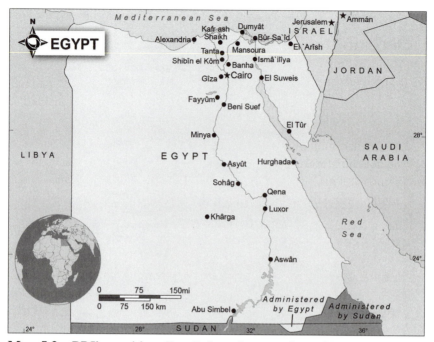

Map 5.2   BRI's maritime Road's long journey from China ends in the Mediterranean Sea.

to Uganda, Rwanda and South Sudan.[13] This opens up the countries that have close trading links with Kenya, by giving them access to the BRI.

Kenya's GDP growth has averaged over 5 percent for the last decade. It is the economic, financial, and transport hub of East Africa. The SGR is a flagship project under the Kenya Vision 2030 development agenda by which America's Central Intelligence Agency says Kenya is well placed to resume its decade-long 5 to 6 percent growth rate, of which the SGR will be an integral part. China's BRI inroad ties China to the Kenya Vision 2030 agenda and makes China a visible contributor to Kenya's long-range plan to benefit Kenya's economy, while also providing modern rail technology to three of Kenya's neighboring countries. This is a stepping-stone to connecting even more African countries to the port of Mombasa someday, which will allow them to plug into the BRI and use it to import and export around the world.

DJIBOUTI

From Mombasa, the BRI's maritime route swings around the Horn of Africa and enters the Red Sea through the narrow, 20-mile (32-kilometer) strait of Bab al-Mandeb at Djibouti, a small, impoverished country with high unemployment, but a country that is so strategically located that it is home to the militaries of the United States, China, France, Britain, Italy, Germany, and Japan. A Saudi Arabian base is not far behind. Most of the bases are within short driving distances from one another. Djibouti hosts the only American base in Africa, Camp Lemonnier, and the only Japanese base in the world! America, China, France, and Japan lease their bases from the Djiboutians; Italy and Britain share the American base. France's base hosts the Germans and Italians.[14] In all, about 4,000 U.S. military personnel are stationed in Djibouti; China has approximately 2,000, and Japan 170.

What makes Djibouti so important to all these countries that maintain militaries there is its location on the Horn of Africa, astride the narrow strait that leads to the Red Sea and the Suez Canal, an ancient maritime route that has been plied for centuries to convey commerce from Asia to Europe (see Maps 5.1 and 5.2). Annually, 30 percent of all global shipping passes through this narrow passage.

The place to begin unpacking China's investment in Africa is Djibouti, where the axis of commerce, geopolitics, and the growing competition between the United States and China intersect. From here, the maritime road component of the BRI transits through the Red Sea into the Mediterranean through the Suez Canal, and north to the port of Piraeus in Athens, Greece. BRI's route then continues north until it connects with the belt component of BRI in central Europe.

Recent developments in Djibouti have clearly illuminated the importance of the country to China's strategy of achieving geographically selective military dominance. In this respect, China is playing for high stakes, and from all evidence, is winning.

Djibouti's economy is largely comprised of service activities connected with the country's strategic location as a deepwater port on the Red Sea. Djibouti provides services as both a transit port for the region and an international transshipment and refueling center. Imports, exports, and reexports represent 70 percent of port activity at Djibouti's container terminal. Reexports consist primarily of coffee from landlocked neighbor Ethiopia. Djibouti has few natural resources and little industry. The nation of under one million in population, is therefore, heavily dependent on foreign assistance to support its balance of payments and to finance development projects.

The 100-acre U.S. base in Djibouti, for instance, has some 4,000 troops and a lease of $630 million in 2014, not an insignificant contribution to a country with a gross domestic product of around $2 billion. And Camp

Lemonnier, as the U.S. base is called, is only one of a number of militaries that pay to coexist with each other in Djibouti.[15]

The Djibouti government has emphasized infrastructure development for transportation and energy, and with the help of foreign partners, particularly China, has begun to increase and modernize its port capacity.

In 2017, Djibouti launched two of the largest projects in its history, the Doraleh Port and the Djibouti-Addis Ababa, Ethiopia Railway, the latter funded by China under its Belt and Road Initiative.[16]

The railway line demonstrates the winning hearts and minds aspect of the BRI, but Doraleh Port is a reminder that there is another use for the BRI: furthering China's national interests, through whatever means possible. Here's why.

Djibouti's neighbor, Ethiopia (Map 5.1), is a landlocked country, a severe disadvantage to a nation that needs access to a deep-sea port to import and export 90 percent of its products. The closest port is Djibouti, which is some 466 miles (750 kilometers) from Addis Ababa, the capital of Ethiopia.

Prior to the SGR railway, it took three days for Ethiopia to move its exports to Djibouti. The railway has cut the time to under 12 hours. The $3.4 billion project was 70 percent financed by China's Export-Import Bank and built by China Railway Group and China Civil Engineering Construction. The trains will be operated by Chinese staff for 5 years.

In another first for China, the Addis Ababa-Djibouti railway is the first electrified line in Africa. This is BRI at its best, transforming countries' economies. As Getachew Betru, chief executive of Ethiopia Railways told the BBC, "if you want to bring your container from Hong Kong to Djibouti, it will take you maybe two, three weeks. But it will take you more than that to take it from Djibouti to Addis Ababa. It will now take us one day."[17]

The Doraleh terminal in Djibouti, on the other hand, illustrates the steel that lies within the velvet glove of the Belt and Road Initiative. Although China did not build, nor does it operate the terminal seaport at Djibouti, as it grew in importance to China's national interests, China is poised, it seems, to engineer a forced change in ownership of Doraleh, to itself! This tale of intrigue begins with Djibouti and Abu Dhabi, the capital of the United Arab Emirates.

In the storied history of maritime commerce, Djibouti holds a legendary status. As its own history book tells it: Djibouti as a main maritime passage and a main trading route between East and West stretches back 3,500 years, the time of maritime explorations of the Red Sea. A strategic meeting point between two worlds (Africa and Asia), the Red Sea was a place of contact and passage used by Egyptians, Phoenicians, Ptolemaists, Romans, Greeks, Byzantine, Arabs, and then Europeans in search of the spices route. Its apogee came with Djibouti's strategic location that enabled the port authorities to successfully rise to the challenge of turning the port into a regional hub for the Red Sea and Indian Ocean, and in a wider context, for the three continents of Europe, Africa, and Asia. Containerization was the defining concept behind this new period of development, and Djibouti's first modern container terminal began operations in February 1985, with the opening of Suez Canal."

Container-based commerce revolutionized maritime trade. For the first time, the dimensions of containers were standardized globally. Hundreds (now thousands) of 20- or 30-foot containers could be put on board larger and larger container ships. As the gantry crane technology developed, loading and unloading containers fast became the core differentiator between world-class ports and the also-rans. Among the handful of far-thinking ports that invested in container-handling technology was Abu Dhabi, capital of the United Arab Emirates.

A small local port operator, Abu Dhabi, through its vision and entrepreneurial skill grew to become, in its own words, a "global trade enabler," with a team of over 36,000 people working at more than 78 terminals around the world today. With a name befitting its new role, DP World, Abu Dhabi is now one of the world's most efficient port managers and owns or leases properties that include 78 businesses in 40 countries, employs 450,000 people, serves 70,000 vessels annually, and moves 174,000 containers every day. The UAE is a strong ally of the United States to boot.[18]

One of DP World's customers was the port of Doraleh in Djibouti. DP World made major improvements at Doraleh after it signed the 20-year concession in 2000 to operate the port. Then, the unexpected happened—the lease was terminated unilaterally by Djibouti in 2011!

It turned out DP World had signed on a new client, a port at Berbera in Somaliland, which is adjacent to Ethiopia. The deal posed a potentially fatal threat to Djibouti's role as the main export/import conduit for Ethiopia and could also adversely impact Djibouti's role as the main point of entry for goods from Asia in the long term.

After Djibouti cancelled the DP World concession, it turned to China to make major improvements to the port of Doraleh; I suspect the fact that it was replacing a long-time American ally was icing on the cake! China was only too glad to underwrite the expansions and improvements, and six years later the Doraleh Multi-Purpose Port, refurbished by China, opened for business. In addition to the improvements China intends to implement, other projects in Djibouti including a free-trade zone, upgrading old docks and constructing yet another industrial zone.

Now, as the payment stream to pay off the loans that Djibouti has borrowed from Chinese companies begins, there are early rumors that the payments will be too high for Djibouti's small economy. And BRI skeptics are already pointing out that this is an ominous development for Djibouti because it seems headed to a similar fate as the port of Hambantota, Sri Lanka, as described earlier in this book.

When Sri Lanka could no longer meet its contractual obligations to China, the friendly neighborhood infrastructure builder transformed itself into a tough bill collector and wound up owning the port of Hambantota. If this scenario played out in Doraleh, it would be an ominous development. China could block the transport of U.S. military supplies into Djibouti, and that would close the curtain for U.S. military presence, not just in Djibouti, but also in Africa, given that no other African country appears ready to accept a U.S. military base on its soil.

Whether these dire projections are accurate remains to be seen, but they were serious enough for U.S. Security Adviser John Bolton to raise a warning flag in December 2018, and alert the world community that China was poised to take control of the port.[19]

"Handing over the operation of the port would not only allow China to constrain operations at Camp Lemonnier," Reuben Brigety, former U.S. ambassador to the African Union told the *Washington Post*. "It would also have economic consequences in the region." The ports in Djibouti are a major transit point for goods shipped to Ethiopia, Africa's second most populous country, and Djibouti, at the southern end of the Red Sea, is on the shipping route between Asia and the Suez Canal. Every day, an estimated 4.8 million barrels of oil transit through the strait adjacent to Djibouti. "The United States is asleep at the switch while all of this is happening," Brigety warned.[20]

If the United States is forced to close its military base in Djibouti, it will end the antiterrorism and intelligence operations that America carries out from the country and leave China as the only superpower in this strategic corner of the world. It would be a major loss for America's military plans and its national security operations around the Horn of Africa. It would also affect U.S. national interests elsewhere in Africa because, for instance, the United States conducts secret Special Forces missions and drone strikes against terrorist cells in Somalia and other African countries. A somber scenario indeed!

After Djibouti, oceangoing Chinese vessels enter the Red Sea and then pass through the Suez Canal, Egypt, finally exiting into the Mediterranean Sea, and head to the Greek port of Piraeus, which is also controlled by China, is a key BRI node, and is increasingly China's portal into Europe.

EGYPT

"Egypt and China are countries with ancient civilizations. . . . We were connected in the past by the maritime Silk Road which reached Alexandria," Liu Wei, president of Renmin University in China told *Xinhua*, referring to the port city in northern Egypt, on January 13, 2019, as he and Egypt's Ain Shams University inaugurated the Belt and Road Cooperation Research Center in the Egyptian capital Cairo.[21] "I hope this center will be a bridge linking Egypt and China for increasing cultural and economic ties," Liu said.

Inauguration of the Belt and Road Cooperation Research Center was a capstone moment for both China and Egypt, as their BRI involvement has deepened by the year. Egypt's Suez Canal is itself a critical part of the world's commercial infrastructure, as it sits at the focal point of commerce between Africa, the Arab world, and the Middle East (see Map 5.2). It connects the continents of Africa and Asia, is an Asian portal for the African and Arab worlds, and an African portal for Europe through the Mediterranean Sea.

Goods and services produced in Egypt enter customs-duties free into European markets and Arab countries' common market, and most Egyptian products enter duty and tariff free to the United States. Egypt is now home to over 1,500 Chinese companies that have made about $610 million in investment, excluding the Suez Canal zone, and have created 27,566 jobs.[22]

Under the BRI, China has financed the Suez Canal Economic Zone (SCZone) to upgrade several ports and to improve infrastructure for expanding the Egyptian economy. Dozens of Chinese companies currently invest in the Suez Canal region, including Chinese industrial developer Tianjin Economic-Technological Development Area (TEDA), which is developing an area of 7.23 square kilometers in the SCZone. The development has already attracted dozens of companies, including China's fiberglass manufacturing giant Jushi, which has helped Egypt become one of the largest producers and exporters of fiberglass in the world.[23]

According to Liu Aimin, president of TEDA, "About 70 different companies have settled in the industrial zone, like China Power Tianjin New Energy Development Co., China Glass Holdings, China Shipping, and Joshi Fiberglass. With the contracted investment of nearly $1 billion in 2017, annual sales of about $180 million and foreign trade (imports and exports) of $290 million, TEDA provides nearly 3,000 jobs."[24]

Besides the Suez Canal, Egypt's importance lies in its size, economic heft, and influence wielded in the Arab world. With a population close to 100 million and a GDP of around $1.2 trillion, Egypt is both an important commercial partner for China and a growing facilitator of trade links between China, Israel, and Turkey. Or as President Xi Jinping would proudly say, Egypt is a living testament to the BRI's core philosophy of creating win-win partnerships.

Besides the three African countries that lie directly in the path of the Belt and Road Initiatives, dozens of projects are being funded under the BRI brand. Most of these are included in the Appendix. As I mentioned earlier, this chapter's aim was to focus on the strategic and economic impact of the BRI's maritime route as it completes its long journey from China to Europe along the Horn of Africa through the Suez Canal. I would like to summarize some of these far-flung projects[25] and speak to the growing concept of a BRI brand before we turn to conclusions and recommendations for a U.S. response to BRI.

PORT SUDAN TO KHARTOUM RAILWAY

Analogous to the Kenyan project that connects Mombasa to the country's inland capital of Nairobi, the Port Sudan to Khartoum rail line connects South Sudan's main port to its capital. This gives the BRI's maritime route access to yet another country through its main port for both imports and exports, either from China or any of the Asian ports touched by the BRI during its east-west transit to the Athenian port of Piraeus. And in reverse from Piraeus to Asia.

The project is worth $1.3 billion, a sizeable amount given that South Sudan's gross domestic product in 2017 was $20 billion. It was signed on February 28, 2007, between Sudan and two Chinese companies, China Railway Engineering Group Co., Ltd. and China Railway Erju Co., Ltd. It was funded by the Chinese government through export credits. The project was completed in 2012, and connects Port Sudan to the country's capital, Khartoum, in 475 miles (762 kilometers) of rail network.

The government of South Sudan relies on oil for the vast majority of its budget revenues. South Sudan is one of the most oil-dependent countries in the world, with 98 percent of the government's annual operating budget and 80 percent of its GDP derived from oil.[26]

Oil is exported through a pipeline that runs to refineries and shipping facilities at Port Sudan on the Red Sea, which makes the Port Sudan to Khartoum's Belt and Road Initiative project a critical part of South Sudan's infrastructure, and increasingly ties the country's future development to China.

MALAWI—INFRASTRUCTURE PROJECTS

China has funded $1.7 billion worth of infrastructural projects in this southern Africa country. The deal includes a 300-megawatt coal-powered station at Kam'mwamba worth $667.2 million, and reconstruction of the Chileka International Airport at a cost of $285.4 million. Others are the 87-mile (140-kilometer) Tsangano-Mwanza (in Tanzania) road construction worth $169.4 million, upgrading of the Phombeya-Makanjira-Nkhotakota-Chatoloma 220 kV power line worth $189.3 million, and $23 million to fund construction of the Blantyre District Hospital and Cancer Centre.

MOZAMBIQUE—MPHANDA NKUWA DAM AND HYDROELECTRIC STATION PROJECT

Worth $3.1 billion, the deal was signed by the Mozambican government and Export-Import Bank of China on April 21, 2006. The project upon completion would provide 1,500 megawatts of power to the national electricity grid of Mozambique. The project also covers the construction of Moamba-Major Dam that will supply drinking water to residents of Maputo.

NIGERIA—DANGOTE CEMENT PLC EXPANSION

The deal was signed between Africa's biggest cement producer, owned by the continent's richest man, Aliko Dangote, and Sinoma International Engineering Co., Ltd., a Chinese construction company. It is worth $4.34 billion. The project is an expansion of the Dangote Cement PLC into Nigeria, Ethiopia, Kenya, Zambia, Senegal, Mali, Cameroon, and the Ivory Coast.

This will increase cement production by 25 million metric tonnes, and boost the overall production to over 70 million metric tonnes annually.

CHAD—SUDAN RAILWAY

This project is worth $5.6 billion. It was signed by the government of Chad and China Civil Engineering Construction Corporation on March 14, 2014. The 835-mile (1,344-kilometer) railway is being constructed in three phases and will also link the two nations with Cameroon. Its constructions started in October 2014. China Export-Import Bank has funded $2 billion, with the rest coming from other Chinese government lending institutions.

DEMOCRATIC REPUBLIC OF THE CONGO—INFRASTRUCTURE FOR MINES BARTER DEAL

This deal was signed on September 17, 2007, between the Democratic Republic of the Congo government and China. It is worth $6 billion and is funded by China's Exim Bank. The deal was to develop the minefields in Mashamba and Dima basins and Kolwezi. In return for the loan, the Democratic Republic of the Congo government was to give copper mines, with approximately 10.6 million tonnes of copper, for exploration and mining by Chinese companies.

SOUTH AFRICA—MODDERFONTEIN NEW CITY PROJECT

The Modderfontein New City Project, is being built on the outskirts of the country's capital, Johannesburg. The project, worth $7 billion, is one of the biggest real estate projects undertaken by a Chinese firm in South Africa. A Chinese company, Shanghai Zendai, is building the city, which will become home to at least 10,000 residents upon completion. The city will have finance and trade facilities, an industrial zone, sports and recreation facilities, and an African heritage theme park.

TANZANIA—BAGAMOYO PORT

This project is worth $7 billion. It is funded by China Merchants Port Holding International and the Oman government's State General Reserve Fund. The port is being built in Bagamoyo, a coastal town in Tanzania. It will be able to handle about 20 million containers annually and will be the largest port on the East African coastline, bigger than the port of Mombasa in Kenya. Its construction started in October 2015, but was halted earlier this year due to financial constraint facing the Tanzanian government.

NIGERIA—COASTAL RAILWAY

This is the largest-ever contract awarded to a Chinese company in Africa. The project is worth $12 billion. The deal was signed between the Federal Republic of Nigeria and the China Railway Construction Corp (CRCC) on November 19, 2014. The railway is 871 miles (1,402 kilometers) in length. Upon completion, it will link Lagos, the nation's economic capital, with the eastern city of Calabar, passing through 10 states. It will also link cities with the oil-rich state of Niger Delta.

Over the last decade, China has risen to become the single largest trade partner for many African countries. It has also become a major source of financial support for various development projects being undertaken on the continent.

Infrastructure development is a key pillar of the China-Africa relationship. In Africa, infrastructure projects awarded to Chinese companies are financed by their government through loans and grants.

THE BRI BRAND

As personal computers (PCs) were beginning to proliferate during the 1970s, Intel, the electronic chip manufacturer, came out with a novel marketing campaign. PCs became possible because electronic chip manufacturing technology was able to put virtually all the circuitry that powered a PC on a single chip. Ipso facto, buying the best, most advanced computer chip meant consumers were buying the best computer. Recognizing that millions of nontechnical customers would want to try and figure out which of dozens of brands of PCs they should buy, Intel developed a pitch to establish itself as the most innovative, high-technology, quality electronic computer chip maker in the world. Thus was born the "Intel Inside" campaign, through which Intel dominated the PC industry for over two decades. We don't care what computer you buy, as long as it has an Intel chip inside, customers were told through extensive ad campaigns, educational forums, and trade-show displays.

Even though Intel chips had been used in PCs for years prior to the campaign, the "Intel Inside" campaign absorbed all the previous marketing efforts into a sleek new way of linking Intel's chips with the world's best computers. The message was clear: Do not worry about what brand of computer you buy, as long as you see the "Intel Inside" label on it, you are buying the best. Consumers got the message.

President Xi Jinping has surely taken a leaf from Intel's playbook. The word BRI is now used and understood around the world as China's innovative and visionary project to help build infrastructure around the world using China's cash, expertise, and personnel resources. It is associated with China's efforts to help raise living standards around the world and help countries leapfrog development into richer, middle-class countries by following the model that helped modernize China. All prior Chinese infrastructure development projects in other countries are being increasingly absorbed under the BRI label.

Projects in Africa particularly illuminate this point. Even though China's foreign direct investment into Africa and its efforts to help Africa develop by building up its infrastructure go back years before the 2013 announcement of the Belt and Road Initiative. All those projects are now being increasingly viewed under the BRI umbrella.

Each such connection adds to the image of BRI, and together the hundreds of projects now being executed under the BRI label increasingly create the image of China as the world's leader in infrastructure technology and construction expertise. Perhaps the next step in the Belt and Road Initiative's global branding will be a BRI stamp of approval on every project that was executed under the BRI umbrella! A plaque or lettering chiseled into the project that proudly says "BRI inside," so in the future when countries look for a vendor to develop infrastructure, they will want to make sure and award the winning bid to a vendor that is "BRI approved."

SIX

Toward an American Grand Strategy for China

"The greatest victory is that which requires no battle."
—Sun Tzu, *The Art of War*

It is sheer coincidence, but serendipitous nevertheless, that this book's last chapter is being started on December 18, 2018, the 40th anniversary of the market reforms triggered by President Deng Xiaoping and that catapulted China from an also-ran economy to a superpower.

As this book has recounted, China has much to celebrate as it views its accomplishments during the last four decades, capped with the five-year-old Belt and Road Initiative that has the potential to expand China's commercial alliances to more than 70 countries. Already, under the auspices of the BRI, Chinese companies have built 82 economic and trade cooperation zones in 24 countries along the Belt and Road Initiative routes; the BRI has created more than 240,000 jobs; China and the BRI countries have done over US$5 trillion in trade during the five years since the BRI was announced; and over 11,000 freight trains now operate between China and Europe, linking nearly 100 cities across the region.[1]

But, as the *Wall Street Journal*[2] reminds us, the celebrations that begin today are tinged with an unusual amount of discord within China, which looks like it might rub the gloss off today's anniversary. Much of it is directed at President Xi Jinping, not for the country's economic and commercial success, but for his aggressive foreign policy and his no-holds-barred economic drive to catapult ahead of the United States. This drive includes accusations of widespread hacking of intellectual property from U.S. companies to help China leapfrog America's leadership in technologies, such as artificial intelligence and quantum computing, that will become the backbone of the twenty-first-century's commerce, job creation, and military dominance.

"In the weeks leading up to Tuesday's 40th anniversary celebrations, Mr. Xi's brand of forward-leaning foreign policy and strongman-led national development has drawn fire. Critics within the party are pointing to China's flagging economy and down-spiraling relations with the U.S. as proof Mr. Xi has concentrated too much authority in his hands, made policy missteps and provoked pushback against China's superpower ambitions abroad," stated the *Wall Street Journal*. This is a stark reminder that China's future success may not be as smooth as it has been for the last 40 years.

Most of this book has talked about China's three-step grand strategy, and I've argued that, by and large, this visionary strategy has, so far, been executed with deftness and precision. But the final step of the grand strategy, the all-important reach for global influence with the Belt and Road Initiative, is the make-or-break moment for China's reach for global primacy. It's not just because of the BRI's historically unprecedented size and scope, but also because the West and the United States especially are now aware that the BRI is a zero-sum game for the West. The successful execution of the Belt and Road Initiative implies an impending lock by China on political and economic influence, raw materials, and natural resources of a large part of the world. The zero-sum game may be but a decade or two away.

Complicating this impending global geopolitical transition from a Western-dominated world to an Asian-dominated world is the fact that the United States, still the West's leader, is bereft of its own grand strategy. Grand strategy is typically not held in high esteem in the United States. I recall asking a former White House official in the George W. Bush administration about America's missing grand strategy. "Grand strategy is a concept for academics. It has no place in the real world," was the scornful response. Well, welcome to the real world, China style!

Earlier, I pinpointed some of the fault lines China is now encountering in the execution of its Belt and Road Initiative. But China faces other serious problems, any one of which could impact the BRI's success and thereby damage China's growth and its grand strategy. A few examples:

- The Chinese leadership was really caught on the back foot by the ferocity of President Trump's tariffs on China's exports to the United States and their potential impact on China's economy. *Bloomberg News* quotes UBS, the Swiss banking giant, as estimating that the initial round of tariffs on US$50 billion of imports could lower China's economic growth by 0.1 percent in the first year. If the United States imposes tariffs on a further $100 billion of goods, the drag on growth could be 0.3 to 0.5 percent.[3] What might this mean for the $1 trillion investment that China has earmarked for the Belt and Road Initiative?

- Even though China has moved 750 million people from poverty to the middle class during the last 40 years, a recent Peking University report found that China has one of the world's highest levels of income inequality, with the richest 1 percent of households owning a third of the country's wealth. The poorest 25 percent of Chinese households owns just 1 percent of the country's total wealth, the study found. This inequality is compounded by the income differentials between the booming economies of China's coastal cities—the export engines of China—and the provinces, especially the cities of western China. Might these income gaps lead to instability in China as those left behind read about rising living standards in the Belt and Road Initiative countries?[4]

- The well-known bank economist George Magnus, research Associate at Oxford University's China Centre and previously the chief Economist at UBS, warns that the size of China's debt and the speed with which it has accumulated it make China a prime candidate for future instability. He refers to a recent International Monetary Fund (IMF) report that looked at the credit gaps of 45 countries (credit as a share of gross domestic product) and found that when the gap reached 30 percent or more in a five-year period, all but five countries experienced a financial crisis, a sharp slowdown in growth, or both. China's credit gap reached 30 percent in 2016—certainly not a good omen for China's global ambitions, which is clearly reflected in the subtitle of Magnus's recently published book, *Why Xi's China Is in Jeopardy.*[5]

- Last, but not least, is the issue of internal instability in the context of billions of dollars worth of investment that the BRI will need each year in the face of a slowdown in China's economic expansion. In fact, the 6.6 percent growth rate for 2018 reported on Monday, January 21, 2019, is the slowest annual rate since 1990. "The official jobless rate ticked up to 4.9% last month from 4.8% in November."[6]

I could go on. Add these internal issues to the highly publicized accusations of rapacious lending practices, exploitation of local workers, use of Chinese contractors and highly paid consultants, and China's Belt and Road Initiative would seem to have a diminishing chance of success. Sooner or later, the countries that are part of the BRI will see through the shell game that it is and refuse to go along. And that will be the end of Xi Jinping's glorious vision of stitching 70 countries to China in one seamless web of commerce and connectivity. This will inevitably lead to the collapse of China's grand strategy to achieve global primacy.

But it would be wrong to conclude that China's grand strategy will fail, even with the serious potholes China is encountering on its road to implement the Belt and Road Initiative. For one thing, with the success of the first two parts of its unfolding grand strategy—to get rich and to attain military superiority around its coastline—China has already demonstrated its ability to deal with multiple and complex geopolitical, financial, and security issues. And there is no reason to believe China cannot continue to do that in the future.

But more important, a prediction of China's failure as its BRI execution hits roadblocks assumes that its grand strategy is cast in stone—that having formulated an execution plan, it is committed to following that plan into the future, irrespective of global developments. This assumption is incorrect. In fact, exactly the opposite is true.

The essence of a country's successful grand strategy is the country's ability to duck and weave and to adapt to changing realities, while never losing sight of the end goal. Consider America's Cold War grand strategy to contain the Soviet Union. This strategy took four decades to succeed and went through multiple iterations before its ultimate success.

"When Americans think of grand strategy, they often think of terms like 'containment,' the organizing principle that guided U.S. policy for decades. But as [Yale University, Cold War historian] John Lewis Gaddis has pointed out, containment was not a single forty-five-year grand strategy but rather a string of several distinct grand strategies that took varying approaches to the overriding problem of taming Soviet power. As circumstances changed and new problems arose, American grand strategy evolved as well. . . . Grand strategy occurs in a world where almost nothing sits still, so the calculations underlying grand strategy must inevitably shift as well. . . . In this sense, grand strategy requires not just a capacity for systematic thinking but also flexibility and an ability to adapt."[7] As Deng Xiaoping put it, "cross the river by feeling the pebbles," a parable that embodies the essence of grand strategy.

If it seems that I have preordained the success of China's grand strategy, I have not. For, also embodied in Deng Xiaoping's words is an assumption—that feeling the pebbles will *ipso facto* force a course correction. They may not. Having crossed a large part of the river, with the distant shore now in sight, it could be easy to conclude that a cut or bruise from some pebbles does not matter. The accusation, for instance, that the Belt and Road Initiative is really a neocolonialist enterprise rife with predatory lending practices, opaque contracts, shoddy standards, and insensitive use of Chinese workers, even if not completely accurate, is no cause for a course correction. Such overconfidence and hubris would dramatically change the odds of the BRI's success.

In fact, this fork in the road is being tested even as I write this chapter. According to a January 2, 2019, report from *Invests,* "China is said to be on the verge of seizing Kilindini Harbor, the only international seaport in Kenya and the biggest port in east Africa, due to Kenya's failure to pay massive loans it incurred as a partner in China's neocolonialist Belt and Road Initiative (BRI). . . . [T]his will come about if the KPA fail to re-pay a multi-billion Kenya shilling (KSh) loan from China for the construction of a train line known as the Standard Gauge Railway (SGR) between Mombasa and Nairobi. Among the assets to be seized by China is Mombasa's massive Kilindini Harbor, which was listed as among collateral pledged for the SGR. The Kenyan government has not made public the terms of the many deals it has struck with China that are part of the BRI."[8] If China goes through with this forfeiture, to me it would mean that it has taken the wrong fork in the road, no matter the legal justification for the seizure or the naval security considerations of China owning a key port on the Indian Ocean.

A U.S. GRAND STRATEGY

If you should take one thing away from this book, it is the need for the United States to craft a grand strategy to guide its relations with China's Belt and Road Initiative. The gulf between American and Chinese understanding of the BRI was brought home to me during a recent conversation in Canada with the head of a small business accounting firm. He is Chinese and had asked me about the book I was writing. When I told him what it was about, he said it was badly needed because, "With the BRI Beijing is looking decades ahead, while in Washington they think only of the next election cycle." I would challenge you to walk into an America-based accounting firm, besides the big international ones, and quiz its senior management about the BRI. A wall of blank faces is likely to ask, What in the world is that? Yet, the Belt and Road Initiative has the potential to transform geopolitics and commerce and move their center of gravity eastward to Asia. As Parag Khanna, a leading geopolitical expert puts it, "Those who are used to an America First dynamic need to prepare for a world that is now 'Asia First,' and embrace the new Asian system taking shape."[9]

Discount Khanna's forecast by half, and one is still left with the inescapable need to understand and then plan to deal with the Belt and Road Initiative, the engine of this transformation.

But what might a U.S. grand strategy for dealing with China look like, and what might be its essential building blocks? And where and how does one start to build this strategy?

A good place to start might be to think about the boundary conditions that must be satisfied with any proposed U.S. grand strategy. A boundary condition is a mathematical concept—a condition that must be met before attempting to solve a complicated problem with many possible solutions. Boundary conditions help you increase the odds that a solution is correct.

As I see them, in no particular order, the boundary conditions that the construction of a U.S. grand strategy for China must satisfy are:

1. China will become the richest and most commercially influential country in the world within two decades at most. The United States will be in second place. The Belt and Road Initiative will continue to be the engine that drives China to its preeminent influential position.

2. In the 21st century, Asia will be the region of fastest growth in the world.

3. The nations of Asia, in which I include Australia, New Zealand, Japan, and India will be inexorably linked to China, as planets to the sun. Like planets, these nations will tend to move in elliptical orbits around China, closer to China at times, and farther at others.

4. China will have reached parity, and will likely have bypassed, the United States in high technology.

5. The United States and the European Union will form the other pole of competing power blocs. The EU will limp along without the growth necessary to become a muscular player and will not succeed in developing its own military capability, leaving the defense of Europe to the United States.

6. China will continue to be militarily dominant in Asia, which means China will continue to have the ability (that it has now attained) of destroying any U.S.-led military force that comes close to China.

7. China will continue to be a nuclear power, with warheads and missiles that can destroy the United States. A war between China and the United States would end with the destruction of the world as we know it.

8. China's Belt and Road Initiative will have secured dozens of new commercial alliances for China. Some of these will also be military alliances in the sense that they permit China to use their territory for bases and ports, without China guaranteeing their security.

9. The United States will still be the country with the widest and deepest financial markets in the world, and the U.S. dollar will continue to be the world's premier trading and reserve currency, with renminbi as the second most powerful, displacing the euro.

10. The United States will continue to be militarily dominant around the world, except in the vicinity of China. There, China will reign supreme.

11. American soft power, meaning its power to influence other countries with nonmilitary means, will still outweigh China's soft power.

I believe strongly that China will learn to work around the potholes and fault lines that the Belt and Road Initiative has thrown up as I was writing this book. The predictions of the BRI's failure will be proven wrong. The BRI might have a whole different look to it, but it will not collapse. Increasing amounts of private investment will join and supersede China's $1 trillion "starter financing." Consider the February 7, 2019, resignation of World Bank President Jim Yong Kim, three years before his term was to expire, to join Global Infrastructure Partners, a New York-based private equity firm focused on infrastructure investment. This is yet another indication of money that is going to be made through global infrastructure investment by the private sector as the trillion-dollar Chinese investment in the Belt and Road Initiative sucks in increasing amounts of private investment—a development that Mr. Kim can help his new employer uniquely exploit with his previous experience and connections.

But the BRI has yet another important dimension to it beyond roads, bridges, tunnels, and ports: renewable power sources such as wind and solar. In fact, as the *New York Times* reported, China intends to spend more than $360 billion through 2020 in creating renewable power sources, one of the world's fastest-growing industries. By 2020, China expects to have created more than 13 million jobs in the renewable energy sector.[10] Global Infrastructure Partners is one of the leading financiers of renewable power-generation assets, with a war chest of over $35 billion. No wonder Mr. Kim concluded that joining Global Infrastructure Partners "is the path through which [I] will be able to make the largest impact on major global issues like climate change and the infrastructure deficit in emerging markets."[11]

AN AMERICAN GRAND STRATEGY FOR CHINA

Instead of a well-thought-out grand strategy, the United States seems to have decided that the best way to take on the Belt and Road Initiative is to disparage it, mainly by painting the BRI as one big colonial enterprise. Almost all of the officials in the State Department follow this script, as I discovered in Asia and the United States.

There are finally attempts at competing with China's Belt and Road Initiative by marketing U.S. funding and technology for infrastructure projects. The Trump administration has set up a new foreign aid institution—the United States International Development Finance Corporation with $60 billion of lending authority and insurance for U.S. corporations to encourage them to do business in developing countries.[12]

Vice President Mike Pompeo sweetened the pot a bit by announcing another $113 million in July 2018, at the Indo-Pacific Business Forum in Washington, D.C. The vice president, with pointed reference to the overall U.S. story line of contrasting American largesse to Chinese colonialism, said, "We all want all nations, every nation, to be able to protect their sovereignty from coercion by other countries. . . ." Without mentioning China, he said, "Our engagement excludes no nation." He continued by saying, "Where America goes, we seek partnership, not domination. We believe in strategic partnerships, not strategic dependency."[13]

The good news is the United States appears finally to have decided to compete with China for the hearts and minds of developing nations. But $190 million is a pinprick when put against the trillion-dollar ($1,000 billion) funding that China has allocated for the BRI. And absent a long-term, well-financed strategy, it is doubtful the U.S. initiative will have any significant impact. Even if there were bipartisan agreement to take on China's BRI with a well-thought-out, massively funded initiative. And no such response is likely, given the state of affairs in Washington, D.C.

SO WHAT ABOUT AN AMERICAN GRAND STRATEGY FOR CHINA?

My thoughts on crafting an American grand strategy for China are that it should be constructed around building blocks that play to America's strengths, attenuate its weaknesses, leverage opportunities, and sidestep potential threats, while satisfying as many as possible of the boundary conditions previously listed. With that in mind, let me offer one suggestion for defining a U.S. grand strategy—a visionary, multiyear project to incrementally tie the United States and China together.

MAKE AMERICA'S INFRASTRUCTURE GREAT AGAIN— JOIN THE BELT AND ROAD INITIATIVE

That America's infrastructure is in dire straits is no secret. Using data from the American Society of Civil Engineers (ASCE), the *Wall Street Journal* recently reported that over 9 percent of the nation's bridges require significant maintenance, rehabilitation, or replacement, at an estimated cost of $123 billion. America's highways need another $713 billion to fix a backlog of upgrades and repairs. And some 6 billion gallons of *treated* water a day are lost due to leaking pipes. Arriving in Singapore's gleaming Changi Airport from JFK, New York's aging airport, Rachel, the heroine of the recent movie, *Crazy Rich Asians,* bursts out in wonder at Changi's butterfly garden and movie theater, "JFK is just salmonella and despair!" she exclaims—a comment with which legions of international travelers will surely agree.

The American Society of Civil Engineers (ASCE) estimates that it will cost approximately $4.5 billion a year over 10 years to repair and upgrade America's infrastructure. Of this, $2.5 billion can be raised on the federal and state levels, leaving an infrastructure funding gap of $2 billion annually—a sizeable investment that America has so far been unwilling or unable to put together. Yet not changing the nation's infrastructure is not an option because, in ASCE's words, "Infrastructure's condition has a cascading impact on our nation's economy, impacting business productivity, gross domestic product (GDP), personal income, and international competitiveness."

Is there a way out of this quagmire? I believe there is: China's $1 trillion infrastructure project that is transforming the roads, bridges, tunnels, ports, energy, and internet connectivity in 70 countries. As part of his ongoing trade negotiations with China, the president should find a way to join the Belt and Road Initiative to harness China's infrastructure edge and the BRI's savings to taxpayers.

The BRI started out with funding from China, but is now increasingly attracting investment from some of the world's largest international banks and consulting firms, which are eager to make money as the BRI matures into the largest infrastructure project in history. Before I hear shouts of "that's a nonstarter" from skeptics, let me point out that the United States is already participating in the BRI in all but name!

When Boston set out to replace its aging Massachusetts Bay Transportation Authority (MBTA) commuter railroad cars, it discovered there were no U.S. manufacturers of railway cars. After an international tender, the city chose China Railway Rolling Stock Corporation (CRRC) from a list that included some of the world's leading companies, including Canada's Bombardier and Japan's Kawasaki. Richard Davey, then Massachusetts' secretary of transportation who helped negotiate the bid and selection of CRRC, told me that "not only was CRRC the low bidder by far (for instance, Kawasaki bid $905 million to CRRC's $566.6 million), it stood out for the quality of its product and its record of completing projects on time."

To accomplish this, CRRC rebuilt a shuttered railcar manufacturing plant in Springfield, Massachusetts, where the assembly of the cars takes place. This factory has created over 200 jobs, with more to be added as the MBTA cars are completed and the factory moves on to build cars for CRRC's new contracts, including 45 double-decker train cars for Philadelphia and 64 new subway cars for Los Angeles, with an option for 218 more. Thirty-three employees are being trained in China as part of the deal. So, together with getting its taxpayers a deal, Massachusetts is well on its way to establishing a transit railcar industry in the commonwealth. In fact, absent political considerations, the United States would already qualify as being a part of China's Belt and Road Initiative!

So, I would suggest that President Trump propose to China's President Xi Jinping that America would welcome China's help in rebuilding America's infrastructure, under the right conditions, of course, to safeguard America's security interests. I am sure Xi Jinping would welcome this opportunity to partner with America, given that the BRI is now part of China's constitution and one of the Chinese president's marquee initiatives. What makes my suggestion timely is that U.S. private equity firms, such as the Blackstone Group, KKR, Stonepeak Infrastructure Partners, and I Squared Capital, are raising large amounts of money to invest in U.S. infrastructure projects. The firms collectively raised $68.2 billion in the first three quarters of 2018.

If the United States were to boldly take this leap to join the Belt and Road Initiative, both President Trump and President Xi Jinping could claim victory in a surefire win-win deal that may also help tone down their rapidly escalating trade war. But the biggest winners would be the American people and the U.S. economy. The intractable but critically important problem that has bedeviled the country for years—how to find the money, technology, and resources to repair and upgrade American infrastructure—would be permanently resolved.

More importantly, if such a deal could be worked out, who knows where it might lead? The business of America, after all, is business, and so is it with China. The two superpowers disagree on many issues, but making money is not one of them.

Kishore Mahbubani, the high-profile Singaporean diplomat and former dean of the Lee Kuan Yew School of Public Policy, is fond of saying that from the year 1 to the year 1820, the two largest economies in the world were China and India. The last 200 years of European and American dominance were an aberration, Mr. Mahbubani says provocatively, "All aberrations come to a natural end."

These days, many seminars and panel discussions end with the question: Is this China's century? Often questioners ask for a show of hands to get the audience's response. The last time I asked the question was as moderator of the China panel at the 2018 World Leadership Forum, the Foreign Policy Association's signature event held each September in New York. Of over a hundred attendees in the room, around a dozen thought that this was China's century!

My own answer to the question is, yes, this is China's century, but it is also America's century. Unless the two countries want to blow up each other, and probably end life on Earth, they must learn to coexist. There is no other choice. And to do that, America must develop a grand strategy for dealing with China—a carefully prepared strategy that may have to last for decades, as did the 40-year "containment" strategy that finally toppled the Soviet Union; perhaps the only time an empire was toppled without a war.

The U.S. strategy must be visionary. It needs to appeal to the imagination of the American people and have the power to transform America's role in the world, just as much as China's Belt and Road Initiative has powered China's transformation and inspired its citizens.

The absence of a grand strategy in response to China's quest for global primacy does not mean that the United States is not responding to the Belt and Road Initiative. It just means America's response is helter-skelter, made up as the situation warrants—a sure recipe for failure. As the Chinese saying has it: If you do not know where you are going, any path will lead you there!

APPENDIX

BRI Projects List

The following is a collection of all known Belt and Road Initiative projects. I say "all known projects" because there appears to be no official Chinese list of BRI projects. This compilation was drawn from the exemplary Reconnecting Asia project website of the Center for Strategic and International Studies (CSIS), with CSIS's kind permission.

AFGHANISTAN

Afghanistan-China–Kyrgyzstan–Tajikistan–Iran Rail Road Project, Afghanistan Section

Funders: Asian Development Bank (ADB): None; The World Bank: None

Total Reported Cost: US$3.2 billion

Begin Date: N/A

End Date: N/A

Contractors: N/A

Description: The project is envisioned to improve regional connectivity and commerce. The 1,305-mile (2,100-km) railway will increase access to China and Iran, including the Chabahar and Bandar-e-Abbas ports.

ALBANIA

Tirana–Dibra Arber Motorway Construction (PPP)

Funders: The Export-Import Bank of China: None USD; Albania Ministry of Public Works Transport and Telecommunications; None USD

Total Reported Cost: N/A

Begin Date: N/A

End Date: 2022

Contractors: China State Construction Engineering Corporation (CSCEC)

Description: The two-lane highway is designed to link the Albanian capital, Tirana, with the isolated Dibra region on the Macedonian border through a shortcut into the mountainous area in central Albania. The segment is expected to be just 16.7 miles (26.8 km) long and aims to shorten the current route by more than 46 miles (74 km), cutting travel time from 4 to 1.5 hours.

Europort Shengjin

Funders: N/A

Total Reported Cost: EUR 1.2 billion

Begin Date: N/A

End Date: N/A

Contractors: China Communications Construction Co., Ltd.; VEGA Construction Group

Description: This project aims to develop the port of Shëngjin as Albania's biggest industrial port. Upon completion, the New Port of Shëngjin will connect the South Adriatic and East Mediterranean with the Central, Eastern, and Northern European countries. It will also allow bypassing the congested Bosporus and Dardanelle Strait by providing alternative access to the Adriatic and Black Seas. With a capacity of 60 Million Tons per year, the port is expected to cater to the connectivity needs of not only Albania, but also its landlocked neighbors like Kosovo, Serbia, and Macedonia.

AUSTRIA

Kosice–Vienna Railway (Construction)

Funders: Slovakia: None USD

Total Reported Cost: EUR$6.5 billion

Begin Date: N/A

End Date: 2033

Contractors: N/A

Description: The "1520mm Broad Gauge-Connection Košice-Vienna" project entails the construction of a 280-mile (450-km)-long 1520-mm broad-gauge railway from Košice through Bratislava to Vienna. Breitspur Planungsgesellschaft mbH, the project company, aims to create a continuous, integrated corridor from China and Russia to central Europe. The construction is estimated to start in 2024, with the railway being operational by 2033.

BANGLADESH

Aminbazar–Azimpur Expressway (Construction)

Funders: Bangladesh: None; China: None; Guizhou No. 2 Power Engineering Construction Company: None

Total Reported Cost: US$524 million

Begin Date: N/A

End Date: N/A

Contractors: Guizhou No 2 Power Engineering Construction Company; Maisha Group

Description: The construction of an expressway between Aminbazar and Azimpur in Bangladesh will be financed through a public-private partnership. In May 2013, Maisha Group and Guizhou signed an MoU to invest in the project.

Chittagong Karnaphuli River Tunnel (Construction)

Funders: The Export-Import Bank of China: None; Bangladesh: BDT $36,472,000,000

Total Reported Cost: US$1.1 billion

Begin Date: 2017

End Date: 2021

Contractors: China Communications Construction Company

Description: The Karnaphuli River Tunnel in the port of Chittagong, Bangladesh, is a proposed 2-mile (3.4-km)-long, 6.2-mile (10-m)-wide tunnel under the river. The project includes approximately 3.7 miles (6 km) of connecting roads, and will connect the port of Chittagong to the industrial area of the city to relieve pressure on the three existing bridges. Sedimentation issues precluded the possibility of building an additional bridge. The tunnel is expected to be completed in 2021, and will be the first of its kind in Bangladesh.

Dhaka–Jessore Railway (Construction)

Funders: Bangladesh: None; China Railway Construction Corporation: None; Export-Import Bank of China: None USD; None Listed: None

Total Reported Cost: US$3.4 billion

Begin Date: N/A

End Date: 2022

Contractors: China Railway Construction Corporation, Ltd.

Description: The Padma Bridge Rail Link (also known as the Dhaka-Jessore Railway) connects Dhaka and Jessore via the Padma Bridge in Bangladesh. In February 2015, the government completed feasibility studies and designing work for the project. In July 2016, the Bangladeshi government granted approval to the China Railway Group to build the rail line, and in August 2016, the China Railway Construction Corporation signed an official construction contract. In February 2018, the Export-Import Bank of China also committed funds for the project. The project is being developed in two phases. The first is a 51-mile (82-km) section from Dhaka to Bhanga, and the second is a Bhanga to Jessore section.

Payra Deep-Sea Port (Construction)

Funders: Bangladesh: None; India: None

Total Reported Cost: US$15 billion

Begin Date: N/A

End Date: 2023

Contractors: China Harbor Engineering Company; China State Construction Engineering Corporation (CSCEC); Jan De Nul Group

Description: This port in Payra, Bangladesh, is partially constructed and began basic operations in August 2016. According to BMI research, the full port construction project will have 19 separate components, 13 of which will be implemented under foreign direct investment, and six of which will be financed through government-to-government deals. The total cost of the port is estimated to be between US$11 and 15 billion. In September 2017, the Bangladesh University of Engineering and Technology won a contract to prepare the master plan and design the port. The China Harbour Engineering Company (CHEC) and China State Construction Engineering Corporation (CSCEC) were awarded contracts worth US$600 million to develop 2 of the 19 components. CHEC will construct the main port infrastructure (terminals etc.), and CSECC will be responsible for riparian aspects, the construction of housing, and health care and education facilities around the port. A coal-based power plant is also being constructed to power the port and port city.

Sitakunda–Cox's Bazar Expressway (Construction)

Funders: Bank of China: None USD

Total Reported Cost: US$2.8 billion

Begin Date: 2019

End Date: 2021

Contractors: China Harbor Engineering Company

Description: The Sitakunda-Cox's Bazar Marine Drive Expressway involves the construction of a 106-mile (170-km)-long marine drive expressway along the coastline of the Bay of Bengal. The seaside expressway will connect Chittagong's industrial hub, Sitakunda, with the sea beach in Cox's Bazar. This expressway will be connected with the Bangladesh–China–India–Myanmar (BCIM) Economic Corridor and Asian Highway 41. The project includes approximately 100 bridges and 50 miles (80 km) of coastal protection works.

3rd Shitalakshya Bridge (Construction)

Funders: Saudi Fund for Development (SFD): None; Bangladesh: None

Total Reported Cost: US$57 million

Begin Date: 2017

End Date: 2020

Contractors: Sinohydro

Description: This project is for the construction of a bridge over the Shital-akshya River to establish a direct connection between Bandar Upazila and the Narayanganj district. Financed by the Saudi Fund for Development and the government of Bangladesh, a contract for the bridge's construction was awarded to Sinohydro in February 2017.

BELARUS

China–Belarus Great Stone Industrial Park (Construction)

Funders: China Development Bank: US$1.5 billion; Export-Import Bank of China: US$1.5 billion

Total Reported Cost: US$30 billion

Begin Date: December 11, 2015

End Date: 2045

Contractors: N/A

Description: Advertised as the "pearl of the Silk Road Economic Belt," the Great Stone Industrial Park will be the largest industrial park in Europe established by China. The park is located 15.5 miles (25 km) east of Minsk, right next to the Minsk National Airport, and will occupy an area of approximately 31 square miles (80 km^2). The project is expected to be completed in about 30 years, although segments of the park will open as they are finished. Belorussian government officials expect to have about 10,000 people working and living in the park by 2020, and more than 130,000 people by 2030. They plan for the project to attract US$30 billion worth of foreign investment and are providing lucrative tax exemptions to lure prospective residents.

Bobruisk–Zhlobin Highway

Funders: Export-Import Bank of China: US$322 million

Total Reported Cost: N/A

Begin Date: August 2014

End Date: June 2, 2016

Contractors: China Communications Construction Co., Ltd.; China Road and Bridge Corporation

Description: Bobruisk-Zhlobin Highway is part of M5/E271 Minsk-Gomel Highway Upgrading and Reconstruction Project. As the result of this infrastructure project, all the roads on the international transport corridors will be able to allow passage of vehicles with the requirements of the EU 96/53/SE with a single-axle load of 11.5 tons. The project will be of great importance to accelerating the formation of Belarus's regional economic pattern, and driving the all-round economic development of towns along the highway.

BOSNIA AND HERZEGOVINA

Banja Luka–Mliniste Highway

Funders: Export-Import Bank of China: EUR$1.4 billion

Total Reported Cost: EUR$1.4 billion

Begin Date: 2018

End Date: N/A

Contractors: Power Construction Corporation of China

Description: The Ministry of Transport and Communications RS says that, according to estimates, the entire project of the highway Banja Luka—Mlinište will cost about EUR$1.4 billion, and that this road, beside the highway Banja Luka—Doboj, is one of the priority routes.

Banja Luka–Novi Grad–Dobrin Rail (Modernization)

Funders: Shandong Hi-Speed Group: None USD

Total Reported Cost: US$640.0 million

Begin Date: N/A

End Date: N/A

Contractors: Shandong Hi-Speed Group

Description: This project was jointly funded with another (the Banja Luka—Prijedor—Novi Grad Highway).

BRUNEI

Muara Container Terminal (Upgrade)

Funders: N/A

Total Reported Cost: N/A

Begin Date: N/A

End Date: N/A

Contractors: N/A

Description: In February 2017, Muara Port Company Sdn Bhd (MPC) started running Muara Container Terminal (MCT), Brunei's largest container terminal, according to Reuters.

BULGARIA

Edirne–Sofia High Speed Rail (Construction)

Funders: N/A

Total Reported Cost: N/A

Begin Date: N/A

End Date: N/A

Contractors: N/A

Description: N/A

CAMBODIA

Takhmao Bridge and Connecting Roads

Funders: China: US$32,890,000

Total Reported Cost: US$32.9 million

Begin Date: July 2011

End Date: August 2, 2014

Contractors: Shanghai Construction Group Co., Ltd.

Description: N/A

Construction of Second Ring Road

Funders: China: None USD

Total Reported Cost: N/A

Begin Date: December 28, 2016

End Date: December 28, 2019

Contractors: N/A

Description: N/A

Ksemksant–Thnal Totueng Road (Expansion)

Funders: Export-Import Bank of China: US$40,880,000

Total Reported Cost: US$40.9 million

Begin Date: March 14, 2017

End Date: March 2020

Contractors: China Road and Bridge Corporation

Description: The renovation project of expanding National Road 51, which links between National Roads 1 and 5, will further alleviate traffic.

Kamchay Hydroelectric Power Plant

Funders: Export-Import Bank of China: US$280,000,000

Total Reported Cost: US$280 million

Begin Date: 2007

End Date: 2011

Contractors: Sinohydro

Description: N/A

National Highway No. 5 Extension Project

Funders: China: US$56,800,000

Total Reported Cost: N/A

Begin Date: May 16, 2013

End Date: August 28, 2016

Contractors: Shanghai Construction Group Co., Ltd.

Description: N/A

Udong–Thnal Totoeng Road (NR 51)

Funders: N/A

Total Reported Cost: US$40.0 million

Begin Date: March 2017

End Date: 2020

Contractors: N/A

Description: N/A

NR 58 Banteay Meanchey–Otdar Meanchey Road (Construction)

Funders: Export-Import Bank of China: US$119,751,775

Total Reported Cost: US$122 million

Begin Date: March 18, 2015

End Date: December 2018

Contractors: Shanghai Construction Group Co., Ltd.

Description: The new road is being built to accelerate economic growth in the countryside near the border with Thailand, and connects Banteay Meanchey Province on the Thai border to Oddar Meanchey Province directly to the east.

Siem Reap–Kampong Cham Road—National Road 6A (Widening)

Funders: N/A

Total Reported Cost: USD$248 million

Begin Date: March 2013

End Date: 2017

Contractors: Shanghai Construction Group Co., Ltd.

Description: In April 2017, 25 miles (40 km) of National Road No. 6A offi-
cially opened to traffic. The road connects Prek Leap commune in
Phnom Penh's Chroy Changvar district to the junction of Kampong
Cham's Batheay district.

Pursat–Thmorda Road (Construction)

Funders: China: US$140 million

Total Reported Cost: US$133 million

Begin Date: May 2015

End Date: August 23, 2018

Contractors: China Road and Bridge Corporation

Description: Prime Minister Hun Sen requested a loan from China for the
development of a 118-mile (190-km) road. The new project, National
Road 55, will branch off National Road 5. This new road will allow for
easier transportation and access to Cambodia's western border with
Thailand.

National Road Project No. 11 (NR1: Neak Loeung—NR7: Thnal Tortoeung)

Funders: China: US$63 million

Total Reported Cost: N/A

Begin Date: 2015

End Date: N/A

Contractors: N/A

Description: National Road Project No. 11 connects the National Road No. 1
and National Road No. 7 from Neak Loeung to Thnal Tortoeung.

Phnom Penh–Sihanoukville Expressway

Funders: N/A

Total Reported Cost: US$1.9 billion

Begin Date: 2017

End Date: 2020

Contractors: China Communications Construction Company

Description: This project is designed for the purpose of connecting Cambodia's capital, Phnom Penh, to the coastal city of Sihanoukville. The estimated length of the expressway will be 118 miles (190 km). The government of Cambodia hopes that the province of Preah Sihanouk will eventually develop into a "multipurpose special economic zone."

Preah Vihear–Kaoh Kong Railway

Funders: Cambodia Iron and Steel Mining Industry Group: None USD; China Railway Group: None USD

Total Reported Cost: US$9.6 billion

Begin Date: July 2013

End Date: 2017

Contractors: China Railway Group

Description: The construction of the Preah Vihear–Kaoh Kong Railway line is a joint venture between two Chinese companies, China Railway Group and Cambodia Iron and Steel Mining Industry Group. The designated rail line is expected to connect a steel plant in Rovieng in Cambodia's northern Preah Vihear Province to the island of Koh Smach in the southwestern province of Koh Kong. Eleven stations will be constructed to run along the designated route, which will run through Koh Kong, Kampong Speu, Kampong Chhnang, Kampong Thom, and Preah Vihear Provinces. The entire length of the route is estimated at 249 miles (400 km).

CHINA
Nizhneleninskoye–Tongjiang Rail Bridge (Construction)

Funders: OJSC Far East Development Fund: RUB$2.5 billion; Petropavlovsk PLC: None; Russia-China Investment Fund: None; Rubicon LLC: None

Total Reported Cost: N/A

Begin Date: N/A

End Date: 2019

Contractors: China Railway Engineering Corporation (CRECG); Giprostroymost Institute; Third Railway Survey and Design Institute Group Corporation

Description: Amur River Rail Bridge project aims to create a new trade corridor between the Nizhneleninskoye Jewish Autonomous Region in Russia and the Heilongjiang Province in China.

Chongqing–Lichuan Railway (Construction)

Funders: Asian Development Bank (ADB): US$1,451,500,000; China Railway Corporation and Chongqing Municipal Government: US$2,530,800,000; China Construction Bank and State Development Bank: US$2,530,800,000

Total Reported Cost: US$4.6 billion

Begin Date: December 29, 2008

End Date: March 3, 2015

Contractors: China Railway Eryuan Engineering Group Co., Ltd.

Description: The project is designed to expand railway network in China's less developed western region and enable connection with the more developed eastern region.

Dali–Ruili Railway (Construction)

Funders: China Railway Corporation: None; Yunnan provincial government: None

Total Reported Cost: CNY$25.7 billion

Begin Date: May 30, 2011

End Date: 2022

Contractors: China Railway No. 17 Bureau Group Co., Ltd.

Description: A part of the Kunming-Singapore Railway and the China-Myanmar Railway, this line connects Dali in Yunnan Province to Ruili on the China-Myanmar border.

Hami–Ejin Railway Ejin–Hami Part (Construction)

Funders: None listed, China assumed: None USD

Total Reported Cost: CNY$9.9 billion

Begin Date: N/A

End Date: December 1, 2015

Contractors: China Railway No. 14 Bureau Group Co., Ltd.

Description: Ejin–Hami Railway is a railway line in western China between Ejin located in western Inner Mongolia and Hami in the eastern region of Xinjiang Province. The railway is part of a rail corridor that will extend from Tianjin, on the Bohai Gulf in North China to Torugart Pass on the border with Kyrgyzstan. The rail shortens the distance from Hohhot to Kazakhstan by over 498 miles (800 km).

G3012 Turpan–Hotan Expressway

Funders: China: None USD

Total Reported Cost: CNY$3.5 billion

Begin Date: N/A

End Date: N/A

Contractors: N/A

Description: N/A

G3013 Kashgar–Irkeshtam Expressway

Funders: N/A

Total Reported Cost: US$43.0 million

Begin Date: N/A

End Date: December 12, 2013

Contractors: N/A

Description: N/A

G314 National Road

Funders: N/A

Total Reported Cost: N/A

Begin Date: N/A

End Date: N/A

Contractors: N/A

Description: N/A

G6 Beijing–Lhasa Expressway

Funders: N/A

Total Reported Cost: CNY$679.0 million

Begin Date: N/A

End Date: 2020

Contractors: N/A

Description: N/A

Golmud–Korla Railway

Funders: N/A

Total Reported Cost: CNY$37.6 billion

Begin Date: N/A

End Date: 2019

Contractors: N/A

Description: N/A

Hefei–Fuzhou Railway (Construction)

Funders: N/A

Total Reported Cost: CNY$109.8 billion

Begin Date: April 27, 2010

End Date: June 28, 2015

Contractors: China Railway Construction Corporation Ltd.; China Major Bridge Engineering; China Railway No. 1 Bureau Group Co., Ltd.; China Railway No. 2 Bureau Group Co., Ltd.; China Railway No. 4 Bureau Group Co., Ltd.; China Railway No. 6 Bureau Group Co., Ltd.; Jing Fu PDL An Hui Co., Ltd.

Description: Hefei–Fuzhou High-Speed Railway is in eastern China and connects Hefei and Fuzhou. It has a total length of 813 kilometers and runs through Anhui, Jiangxi, and Fujian Provinces. The line constitutes a portion of the proposed Beijing-Taipei High-Speed Railway, which would tunnel under the Taiwan Strait from Fuzhou to the island of Taiwan.

Hong Kong–Zhuhai–Macau Bridge (Construction)

Funders: Government of the Hong Kong SAR: CNY\$6.75 billion; Bank of China; Kong-Zhuhai-Macao Bridge Authority: CNY\$22 billion; government of Macau SAR: CNY\$1.98 billion; China: CNY\$7 billion

Total Reported Cost: CNY\$110.0 billion

Begin Date: December 2009

End Date: October 23, 2018

Contractors: Bouygues Group; Dragages; CCCC Highway Consultants Co., Ltd.; China Communications Construction Company (CCCC); Fourth Harbor Engineering Investigation and Design Institute Co., Ltd.; China Harbor Engineering Company; China Road & Bridge Corporation (CRBC); China State Construction Engineering Corporation; Cowi; Gammon Construction Limited; Shanghai Tunnel Engineering & Rail Transit Design and Research Institute; Shanghai Urban Construction Group Corporation

Description: The Hong Kong–Zhuhai–Macau Bridge is the world's longest sea crossing, linking the Hong Kong Special Administrative Region (HKSAR), Zhuhai City of Guangdong Province and Macao Special Administrative Region. It consists of a main bridge in mainland waters together with the boundary crossing facilities, and links roads within the three places. The functions of the bridge are to meet the demand of passenger and freight-land transport among Hong Kong, the mainland (particularly the region of Pearl River West), and Macao, to establish a new land transport link between the east and west banks of the Pearl River, and to enhance the economic and sustainable development of the three places.

Lanzhou–Xinjiang High-Speed Railway

Funders: N/A

Total Reported Cost: CNY$144.0 billion

Begin Date: November 4, 2009

End Date: April 30, 2014

Contractors: China Railway No. 08 Bureau Group Co., Ltd.; China Railway No. 11 Bureau Group Co., Ltd.; China Railway No. 12 Bureau Group Co., Ltd.; China Railway No. 17 Bureau Group Co., Ltd.; China Railway No. 19 Bureau Group Co., Ltd.; China Railway No. 20 Bureau Group Co., Ltd.; China Railway No. 21 Bureau Group Co., Ltd.; China Harbor Engineering Company; China Railway No.13 Bureau Group Co., Ltd.; China Railway No. 16 Bureau Group Co., Ltd.; China Railway No. 18 Bureau Group; China Railway No. 4 Bureau Group Co., Ltd.; China Railway No. 5 Bureau Group Co., Ltd.

Description: The 1,104-mile (1,776-km) Lanzhou-Xinjiang High-Speed Railway is a domestic One Belt, One Road Project that terminates in the city of Urumqi. The project improves transport in the western part of China, near the border with Kazakhstan. It will also connect Urumqi to Beijing by high-speed rail.

Lianyungang Port

Funders: Kazakhstan Temir Zholy: None USD; Lianyungang People's Government: None USD

Total Reported Cost: US$98.0 million

Begin Date: May 2014

End Date: N/A

Contractors: Kazakhstan Temir Zholy; Lianyungang Port Company

Description: The logistics terminal construction project is designed to be a "platform for goods from central Asian countries to go overseas and a boost to the construction of the Silk Road Economic Belt."

Hami–Ejin Railway Linhe–Ejin Part (Construction)

Funders: N/A

Total Reported Cost: CNY$4.3 billion

Begin Date: N/A

End Date: December 26, 2009

Contractors: N/A

Description: Linhe–Ejin Railway is a railway line in western China that links Linhe in western Inner Mongolia and Ejin in eastern Inner Mongolia. The railway, mainly constructed for coal transportation, is part of a Hami-Linhe Railway that connects Mongolia and Xinjiang Province through Inner Mongolia to Beijing.

Manzhouli New International Freight Yard

Funders: China Ministry of Railways; China Railway Container Transport Corp., Ltd.: US$3.3 billion

Total Reported Cost: US$3.3 billion

Begin Date: 2008

End Date: N/A

Contractors: N/A

Description: Manzhouli began to build a new international freight yard in 2008, according to an employee with the Manzhouli land port office. The yard covers an area of 6 square miles (15 km^2) and involved an investment of CNY$3.3 billion in the first phase. It was jointly funded by the Ministry of Railways, the China Railway Container Transport, and other well-known foreign companies. The yard has a railway logistics center, bulk coal, auto, ore, and dangerous chemical yards, as well as a container station. It will help achieve more rational resource allocation at the railway port and have an annual reloading capacity of 70 million tons when put into operation.

Golmud–Lhasa Railway (Construction)

Funders: N/A

Total Reported Cost: CNY$56.0 million

Begin Date: N/A

End Date: July 1, 2006

Contractors: China Railway No. 11 Bureau Group Co., Ltd.; China Railway No. 12 Bureau Group Co., Ltd.; China Railway No. 17 Bureau Group Co., Ltd.; China Railway No. 13 Bureau Group Co., Ltd.; China Railway No. 14 Bureau Group Co., Ltd.; China Railway No. 15 Bureau Group Co., Ltd.; China Railway No. 16 Bureau Group Co., Ltd.; China Railway No. 1 Bureau Group Co., Ltd.; China Railway No. 2 Bureau Group Co., Ltd.; China Railway No. 3 Bureau Group Co., Ltd.; China Railway No. 4 Bureau Group Co., Ltd.; China Railway No. 5 Bureau Group Co., Ltd.

Description: The length of the railway is 1,215 miles (1,956 km). Construction of the 506-mile (815-km) section between Xining and Golmud was completed by 1984. The 710-mile (1,142-km) section between Golmud and Lhasa was inaugurated on July 1, 2006, by Chinese President Hu Jintao. This railway is the first to connect the Tibet Autonomous Region to any other province, which, due to its elevation and terrain, is the last province-level entity in mainland China to have a railway. Passenger trains run from Beijing, Chengdu, Chongqing, Guangzhou, Shanghai, Xining, and Lanzhou.

Quzhou–Ningde Railway

Funders: N/A

Total Reported Cost: CNY$8 billion

Begin Date: 2015

End Date: 2020

Contractors: N/A

Description: The railway line, from Quzhou in Zhejiang Province to Ningde in Fujian Province, will run through Suichang, Longquan, and Qingyuan in Zhejiang and Songxi, Zhenghe, Jian'ou, Pingnan, Zhouning, and Jiaocheng in Fujian. After being opened to traffic, the Quzhou-Ningde Railway, with a projected speed of 99 miles (160 km) an hour, will deliver 40 passenger trains a day in each direction and 60 million tons of cargo per year. The railway will play a significant role in bridging northeast Fujian and outside areas and will facilitate the development of the West Straits Economic Zone.

Sichuan–Tibet Railway (Construction)

Funders: N/A

Total Reported Cost: N/A

Begin Date: December 19, 2014

End Date: 2021

Contractors: N/A

Description: The Chinese government announced the railway link in the 13th Five-Year Plan (2016–20). China's second Tibetan railway after Qinghai-Lhasa Railway, Sichuan-Tibet Railway envisions to connect Tibet's capital Lhasa to China's logistics hub Chengdu.

Xinjiang International Logistics Park

Funders: Port of Duisberg: None USD; None Listed: CNY$1 billion; Urumqi Economic and Technological Development Zone: CNY$4 billion

Total Reported Cost: CNY$5 billion

Begin Date: October 12, 2014

End Date: 2015

Contractors: Xinjiang Land Port Investment Co., Ltd.

Description: This is a logistics park being developed in Urumqi, Xinjiang's Urumqi Economic and Technological Development Zone (10 km from Urumqi's West Railway Station) as part of the One Belt, One Road/Silk Road Economic Belt initiative. The objective is to integrate railways, highways, and air transit in the region. The project broke ground in 2014, and was originally expected to be completed in 2015, but as of July 2016, was still under construction. The logistics park is located on Suzhou Road, extending from North Rail Station to West Rail Station and on to Wangjiagou. Apart from a logistics center, a financial center, business center, and commodity display shopping center will also be built. The project as a whole is called "Natural Future City." This project is part of a citywide initiative ("Urumqi City Logistics Development Plan 2013–2020") to turn Urumqi into a logistical hub for trade with central Asia. Specifically, the plan seeks to increase imports from central Asia and eventually western Europe by adding multilinguistic service hubs and improving logistics technology.

CROATIA

Peljesac Bridge (Construction)

Funders: European Union: EUR$357,284,407; China Road and Bridge Corporation: HRK$2,080,000,000

Total Reported Cost: EUR$651.0 million

Begin Date: N/A

End Date: 2022

Contractors: China Road and Bridge Corporation

Description: The new bridge will connect the Dubrovnik–Neretva County to the rest of Croatia, by crossing the Mali Ston Bay over the Adriatic Sea. This will facilitate a smooth flow of goods and people, especially at the peak of the tourist season, according to the European Commission. The project is vital for the Dubrovnik–Neretva County, which currently lacks direct connection with the rest of Croatia. As it stands now, overland travelers need to pass through a coastal territory of Bosnia and Herzegovina, a non-EU country, to access mainland Croatia, an EU member, thereby passing through two customs checks.

ESTONIA

Nordshore Multimodal Logistics Terminal at Muuga

Funders: China: None USD

Total Reported Cost: N/A

Begin Date: N/A

End Date: N/A

Contractors: N/A

Description: N/A

GEORGIA

Anaklia Deep-Sea Port (Construction)

Funders: N/A

Total Reported Cost: US$2.5 billion

Begin Date: December 2017

End Date: 2021

Contractors: Black Sea Group; Conti International; Van Oord NV

Description: Anaklia Deep-Sea Port will serve as the main gateway for imports for approximately 17 million inhabitants of landlocked Caucasus and central Asian countries and provide critical supply routes for nearly 146 million people living within the port's immediate region. The goal is to serve central Asia and the New Silk Road trade route between China and Europe.

HUNGARY

Budapest–Belgrade High-Speed Railway—Hungarian Section (Construction)

Funders: Export-Import Bank of China: None; Hungarian Development Bank: None

Total Reported Cost: US$2.0 billion

Begin Date: 2020

End Date: N/A

Contractors: N/A

Description: This Chinese-backed high-speed railway is intended to link the capitals of Hungary and Serbia and has been celebrated as a flagship project under China's "16 + 1" format and Belt and Road Initiative. Construction is expected to start in 2020.

Huawei Logistics Centre (Biatorbágy)

Funders: Huawei Technologies Co, Ltd.: None USD

Total Reported Cost: US$1.5 billion

Begin Date: N/A

End Date: 2013

Contractors: N/A

Description: N/A

V0 Budapest Bypass Railway (Construction)

Funders: Export-Import Bank of China: None USD; Hungarian Development Bank: None USD; China Development Bank: None USD; Hungary: None USD; China Railway Construction Corporation, Ltd.: None USD

Total Reported Cost: EUR$1.2 billion

Begin Date: N/A

End Date: N/A

Contractors: Chinese State Railway Company

Description: The primary objective of this bypass is to diminish cargo traffic through Budapest, a fact that excludes the project from certain EU funding sources ("Connecting European Facilities" Transportation Development Fund), due to its domestic focus. The project's acceptance of Chinese funding and construction is somewhat contentious, as China has not allowed mutual investment in the construction of Chinese railways.

INDONESIA

Cirebon–Kroya Rail (Construction)

Funders: N/A

Total Reported Cost: US$105.0 million

Begin Date: May 2017

End Date: 2019

Contractors: PT Kereta Api (Persero)

Description: N/A

Gunturharjo Container Terminal (Construction)

Funders: China Hi-Tech Group Corporation (CHTC): None

Total Reported Cost: N/A

Begin Date: N/A

End Date: N/A

Contractors: N/A

Description: This project is part of China Hi-Tech Group Corporation's $6 billion investment in southern Central Java. The investment includes the container terminal as well as integrated industrial zones in the Wonogiri Regency.

Jakarta–Bandung High-Speed Rail (PPP)

Funders: China Development Bank: US$4.5 billion; PT Kereta Cepat Indonesia–China (KCIC): None

Total Reported Cost: US$5.9 billion

Begin Date: N/A

End Date: 2019

Contractors: China Railway Construction Corporation, Ltd.; China Railway International Group; PT Jasa Marga (Persero) Tbk; PT Kereta Api (Persero); PT Perkebunan Nusantara; PT Wijaya Karya (WiKa)

Description: Jakarta-Bandung High-Speed Rail, one of the Indonesia's first high-speed rail projects, connects Jakarta to Indonesia's second largest city Bandung in West Java. It might be extended later to connect to Surabaya in northeastern Java.

Jakarta Monorail Project, Jakarta (Special City District)

Funders: N/A

Total Reported Cost: US$1.5 billion

Begin Date: N/A

End Date: N/A

Contractors: China Communications Construction Company

Description: The Jakarta city administration decided to cancel its contract with the PT Jakarta Monorail (JM) to develop the monorail routes proposed by the company. According to Jakarta governor, Basuki "Ahok" Tjahaja Purnama, the company did not fulfill at least 15 requirements proposed by the city. The pillars, erected several years ago for the monorail project, were set to be demolished in 2017.

Purukcahu–Bangkuang Rail (Construction)

Funders: N/A

Total Reported Cost: IDR$77.0 trillion

Begin Date: 2018

End Date: 2023

Contractors: N/A

Description: The construction of the Purukcahu-Bangkuang Railway is meant for coal transportation with the capacity of 50 million tons/year. This project has been in the works for nine years and according to Indonesia's Committee for Acceleration of Priority Infrastructure Delivery, the project is yet to receive the Borrow-to-use Permit for Forest Area for the Railway Line from the Ministry of Environment and Forestry.

IRAN

Iran–Armenia Rail Link (Iranian Side) (PPP)

Funders: N/A

Total Reported Cost: N/A

Begin Date: N/A

End Date: 2022

Contractors: N/A

Description: In 2009, Armenia and Iran signed an agreement to construct a railway that would connect Yerevan and Tabriz via Syunik. The total railway line has a length of 292 miles (470 km), and its construction will have an estimated total cost of US$3.5 billion.

Tehran–Mashhad Railway (Electrification)

Funders: Export-Import Bank of China: US$1.5 billion; Iran: US$200 million; China Export & Credit Insurance Corporation (Sinosure): None

Total Reported Cost: US$2.6 billion

Begin Date: N/A

End Date: N/A

Contractors: China National Machinery Imp. & Exp. Corp.; MAPNA Group; Su Power Technology; RZD International LLC

Description: The Tehran-Mashhad line is one of the prioritized railway lines undergoing electrification. With a length of 575 miles (926 km), the Tehran-Mashhad line is one of the most frequented railway lines of Iran and one of the few double-track lines of the country. The highest possible speed on this route is 99 miles (160 km) an hour, which is set to increase to 124 miles (200 km) an hour after the electrification project is completed.

Tehran–Isfahan High-Speed Rail (Construction)

Funders: Iran Bank of Industry and Mine: US$1.8 billion; China: None; China Export & Credit Insurance Corporation (Sinosure): None

Total Reported Cost: US$2.7 billion

Begin Date: February 25, 2015

End Date: 2021

Contractors: China Railway Engineering Corporation (CRECG); Khatam Al-Anbia Construction

Description: The Tehran-Qom-Isfahan High Speed Rail Project is set to cover 233 miles (375 km) with speeds between 186 to 217 miles (300 to 350 km) per hour. This high-speed rail project is one of the major railroad projects Iran is carrying out with the help of international companies, including China Railway Group Limited.

IRAQ

Baghdad–Turkey Highway (Highway No. 2)

Funders: International Monetary Fund: None USD

Total Reported Cost: US$1.2 billion

Begin Date: N/A

End Date: N/A

Contractors: N/A

Description: N/A

ISRAEL

Haifa Bay Port (Construction)

Funders: N/A

Total Reported Cost: ILS$4 billion

Begin Date: 2015

End Date: 2021

Contractors: Ashtrom International Ltd.; Shapir Civil and Marine Engineering

Description: This facility at Haifa Bay is designed to handle 1.86 million TEU per year. The Chinese company, Shanghai International Port Group (SIPG) will operate the facility and has a 25-year contract to do so. The winning bid by SIPG reflects the growing commercial ties between Israel and China.

KAZAKHSTAN

Astana Light Rail

Funders: China Development Bank: US$1.8 billion

Total Reported Cost: US$1.8 billion

Begin Date: May 27, 2017

End Date: 2018

Contractors: ALSTOM Transport SA; Beijing State-Owned Assets Management Company; China Railway International Group

Description: The construction of the Astana Light Rail falls under Kazakhstan's efforts to promote its "Nurly Zhol," or "path to the future" program, and link it to China's Belt and Road Initiative. China Development Bank's loan for the construction of the light rail was signed during Kazakh President Nursultan Nazarbayev's visit to China in 2015. The rail will connect key locations in Astana—the international airport, the expo area, Nazarbayev University, Abu Dhabi Plaza, and the House of Ministries—and will terminate at the new railway Astana Nurly Zhol railway station. It will have 18 stations and accommodate 150,000 people a day.

Khorgos Dry Port

Funders: Kazakhstan Temir Zholy: KZT$40.4 billion; Sovereign Wealth Fund Samruk-Kazyna JSC: KZT$38.4 billion

Total Reported Cost: KZT$78.8 billion

Begin Date: July 2014

End Date: N/A

Contractors: Bazis-A Construction Company; Kalmar

Description: Touted as a "New Dubai" and a "game-changing development," this dry port and logistics center on the Kazakhstan-China border could be a bellwether for other ambitious One Belt, One Road projects.

KYRGYZSTAN

Alternative North-South Highway Kyzyl-Jyldyz–Aral and Karzarm–Jalal-Abad (Rehabilitation)

Funders: Export-Import Bank of China: US$400 million

Total Reported Cost: US$400 million

Begin Date: April 16, 2014

End Date: 2015

Contractors: China Road and Bridge Corporation

Description: This project rehabilitated 96 miles (154 km) of the Alternative North-South Highway in Kyrgyzstan, sections Kyzyl-Jyldyz to Aral (km 183–195) and Karzarman to Jalal-Abad (km 291–433). It is the first phase of a larger, three-stage project that will cost $850 million and construct a 270-mile (433-km) road connecting the Kyrygz cities of Balykchy and Jalal-Abad. The construction of this alternative road will have profound effects on the ability to transport Chinese exports to Uzbekistan, Tajikistan, Kazakhstan, and other surrounding countries through Kyrgyzstan.

Alternative North-South Road Aral–Kazarman (Construction)

Funders: Export-Import Bank of China: US$298.8 million

Total Reported Cost: N/A

Begin Date: 2016

End Date: 2020

Contractors: China Road and Bridge Corporation

Description: This project is the second phase of a three-part project to construct the 270 miles (433 km) Alternative North-South Road through Kyrgyzstan for $850 million. Phase two constructed 60 miles (96 km) of new road, connecting Aral to Kazarman. When the Alternative North-South Road is completed, it will have profound effects on the ability to transport Chinese exports to Uzbekistan, Tajikistan, Kazakhstan, and other surrounding countries through Kyrgyzstan.

Km 9 to 272 of the CAREC Transport Corridor 1 Rehabilitation Project

Funders: The Export-Import Bank of China: US$200 million

Total Reported Cost: N/A

Begin Date: N/A

End Date: Nov. 2014

Contractors: China Road and Bridge Corporation

Description: This project provides for the upgrade and rehabilitation of the Bishkek–Naryn–Tourugart Road from kilometer 9 to kilometer 272.

LAOS

Vientiane–Boten Railway (Construction)

Funders: Export-Import Bank of China: None USD; Laos: None USD; China: None USD

Total Reported Cost: US$5.8 billion

Begin Date: December 25, 2016

End Date: 2021

Contractors: China Railway Group, Ltd.; China Railway No. 5 Engineering Group; China Railway No. 8 Engineering Group; China Railway No. 2 Engineering Group

Description: A part of the Kunming–Singapore Railway, this standard-gauge (1435-mm), 260-mile (420-km) railway goes from Boten, Luang

Namtha Province at the China-Laos border to Vientiane and then Nong Khai Thai-Laos border crossing. It represents a major development to Laos's railway system. A memorandum of understanding (MoU) was initially signed in 2010, between Laos and China, with construction starting in 2016. China Railway Group Limited (CRG), through its subsidiaries, is constructing sections I, II, III, and VI, of the rail line.

Pakbeng–Ngeun Bridge Project

Funders: Export-Import Bank of China: US$29,260,000; Laos: US$1,540,000

Total Reported Cost: US$30.8 million

Begin Date: December 2012

End Date: November 2015

Contractors: China Road and Bridge Corporation

Description: The bridge runs approximately 700 meters long, linking Pakbeng District, Oudomxay Province, and Nguen District in Xayaboury. The Pakbeng-Ngeun Bridge crosses the Mekong River and connects two segments of Laos National Road No. 2 W.

LITHUANIA

Klaipeda Container Port (Construction)

Funders: N/A

Total Reported Cost: N/A

Begin Date: N/A

End Date: 2021

Contractors: China Merchants Group

Description: China Merchants Group plans to build a new outer seaport on the existing Klaipeda Port in Lithuania. The project was first proposed in 2009, but a lack of funding prevented its realization. The port of Klaipeda is a major seaport in Lithuania and could serve as a gateway between the Baltic Sea and Lithuania's landlocked neighbor, Belarus, where China is investing large funds under its Belt and Road Initiative.

MACEDONIA

Kicevo–Ohrid Highway (Construction)

Funders: Export-Import Bank of China: None

Total Reported Cost: EUR$375.0 million

Begin Date: N/A

End Date: June 2021

Contractors: Granit Construction Stock Co.; Sinohydro

Description: Officials between the government of Macedonia and the Exim Bank of China signed a loan agreement on November 26, 2013, wherein a loan would be provided to pay for 10 percent of a new motorway project in Macedonia. On March 22, 2014, construction of the Kicevo-Ohrid Highway began, which will measure 35 miles (56.7) km long, and was to be completed sometime in 2018. The construction of the 33-mile (53-km) Miladinovci–Stip motorway was expected to be completed in May 2017.

Miladinovci–Stip Highway

Funders: Export-Import Bank of China: EUR$206.0 million

Total Reported Cost: EUR$206.0 million

Begin Date: 2014

End Date: September 2018

Contractors: Sinohydro

Description: Officials between the government of Macedonia and the Exim Bank of China signed a loan agreement on November 26, 2013, wherein a loan would be provided to pay for 10 percent of a new motorway project in Macedonia. Beginning on March 22, 2014, construction of Kicevo–Ohrid Highway, which will measure 35 miles (56.7 km) long, was to be completed sometime in 2018 and the construction of the 33-mile (53-km) Miladinovci–Stip motorway was expected to be completed in May 2017.

MALAYSIA

Kuala Lumpur–Tumpat Railway (Construction)

Funders: Export-Import Bank of China: MYR$55 billion

Total Reported Cost: US$13.1 billion

Begin Date: 2017

End Date: 2024

Contractors: China Communications Construction Company

Description: This project entails a 428-mile (688-km) rail track running from Port Klang, Malaysia's main seaport, to Pengkalan Kubor bordering Thailand.

Gemas–Johor Bahru Rail (Double Tracking and Electrification)

Funders: Malaysia: None USD

Total Reported Cost: MYR$8.9 billion

Begin Date: 2016

End Date: 2020

Contractors: China Railway Group, Ltd.; China Communications Construction Company

Description: The Gemas to Johor Bahru Rail is a continuation of the Singapore–Kunming Rail Link. The line will provide Malaysia with electrified tracks that connect to the southern tip of the country.

Melaka (Malacca) Gateway

Funders: N/A

Total Reported Cost: MYR$8 billion

Begin Date: N/A

End Date: 2019

Contractors: N/A

Description: Melaka (Malacca) Port is located 156 km by road from Kuala Lumpur. It is part of a massive urban and resort development project that China and Malaysia are jointly implementing, called the "Melaka Gateway." The Melaka (Malacca) Port construction project is aimed at boosting bilateral trade, shipping, and logistics along China's New Silk Road.

MALDIVES

Male–Hulhule Bridge (Construction)

Funders: Maldives: US$12.6 million; China: US$126 million

Total Reported Cost: US$210 million

Begin Date: December 31, 2015

End Date: 2018

Contractors: CCCC Second Harbour Engineering Company Limited (CCCC2Harbour)

Description: This project involves a bridge connecting Male to the airport island of Hulhule in the Maldives. It was financed through a public-private partnership on a Design Build Finance Maintain Operate (DBFMO) basis.

MONGOLIA

Northern Rail Line Extension, Erdenet–Ovoot–Arts Suuri Rail Line

Funders: Aspire Mining Limited: None USD

Total Reported Cost: N/A

Begin Date: N/A

End Date: N/A

Contractors: China Railway No. 20 Bureau Group Co., Ltd.

Description: N/A

Sainshand–Ereentsav, Nomrog, Bichil Rail Route

Funders: Asian Infrastructure Investment Bank (AIIB): None USD

Total Reported Cost: N/A

Begin Date: N/A

End Date: N/A

Contractors: N/A

Description: The Sainshand–Ereentsav, Nomrog, Bichil (via Hoot) Rail route is a project under the Mongolian Economic Corridor within the larger China–Mongolia–Russia Economic Corridor.

Tavan Tolgoi–Gashuun Sukhait Rail (Construction)

Funders: Shenhua Group: None USD; Sumitomo Corporation

Total Reported Cost: US$1 billion

Begin Date: N/A

End Date: 2020

Contractors: N/A

Description: The Tavan Tolgio Rail Project will link Mongolia's Tavan Tolgoi coal mine to the Chinese border. Mongolia has already invested $200 million but the project needs another $800 million.

Tavan Tolgoi–Sainshand Rail Route

Funders: Asian Infrastructure Investment Bank (AIIB): None USD

Total Reported Cost: N/A

Begin Date: N/A

End Date: 2017

Contractors: N/A

Description: The Tavan Tolgoi–Sainshand Rail route is a project under the Mongolian Economic Corridor within the larger China–Mongolia–Russia Economic Corridor.

MONTENEGRO

Adriatic–Ionian Motorway—Montenegro

Funders: N/A

Total Reported Cost: N/A

Begin Date: N/A

End Date: 2030

Contractors: China Pacific Construction Group

Description: This project is a part of the Adriatic-Ionian Motorway that will stretch across the Balkan Peninsula from Italy to Greece.

Bar–Boljare Motorway (Section of European Motorway XI)

Funders: Export-Import Bank of China: EUR$687 million; government of Montenegro: EUR$120 million

Total Reported Cost: EUR$807 million

Begin Date: N/A

End Date: N/A

Contractors: China Communications Construction Company; China Road and Bridge Corporation

Description: This construction on the Bar-Boljare Motorway is related to the Smokovac–Uvač–Mateševo section. China's Exim Bank and the Montenegrin government are funding the project.

Kolasin–Kos Railway Upgrade (Part of Bar–Belgrade Railway Reconstruction Project)

Funders: European Bank for Reconstruction and Development (EBRD): EUR$5.9 million

Total Reported Cost: N/A

Begin Date: November 25, 2015

End Date: N/A

Contractors: China Civil Engineering Construction Corporation

Description: A subsidiary of China Railway Construction Corporation, the China Civil Engineering Construction Corporation is reported to repair 6 miles (9.86 km) of tracks between Kolasin and Kos in Montenegro.

MYANMAR

Kyaukpyu Deep-Sea Port (Construction)

Funders: N/A

Total Reported Cost: US$7.2 billion

Begin Date: 2016

End Date: N/A

Contractors: Charoen Pokohand Group; China Harbor Engineering Company; China Merchants Holding International Company, Ltd.; CITIC

Group; TEDA Investment Holding; Yunnan Construction Engineering Group

Description: A CITIC Group-led consortium won the tender to build the Kyaukpyu Deep-Sea Port in December 2015. Under the agreement, the CITIC Group will take a 70 percent stake, while the Myanmar government and 42 domestic companies hold the rest. Originally, a $7.2 billion 10-berth port was planned, but later on Myanmar started to renegotiate with the CITIC Group to scale down the project. Construction will be completed in four stages as originally planned but will not proceed to the next phase until certain demand conditions are met. In the first stage, worth roughly $1.3 billion, one wharf capable of mooring two to three ships will be built.

NEPAL

Kalanki–Koteshwor Road (Construction)

Funders: N/A

Total Reported Cost: NPR$5.1 billion

Begin Date: N/A

End Date: Dec. 2018

Contractors: Shanghai Construction Group Co., Ltd.

Description: Construction work to widen the Kalanki–Koteshwor section of Ring Road was likely to be completed within July 2018, a year later than the initially fixed deadline.

PAKISTAN

Chakdara–Kalam Motorway (Widening and Rehabilitation)

Funders: Saudi Arabia: None; Pakistan: None

Total Reported Cost: US$32 million

Begin Date: N/A

End Date: 2018

Contractors: N/A

Description: This motorway project will widen and rehabilitate the highway that is part of the Belt and Road Initiative's China-Pakistan Economic Corridor. To the south, it connects to the Havelian–Abbottabad–Mansehra–Shinkiari–Battagram–Thakot Road. The construction of the road was announced in November 2015, and was expected to be completed in 2018. EA Consulting, a design/architect firm from Pakistan.

Chakdara–Chitral–Shandora–Gilgit Road (Construction)

Funders: China: None; Pakistan: None USD

Total Reported Cost: US$422 million

Begin Date: N/A

End Date: N/A

Contractors: N/A

Description: This CPEC project is in the planning and development phase. It will connect Chakdara in Khyber Pakhtunkhwa to Gilgit in Gilgit-Baltistan via Chitral and Shandora. In September 2017, the project was officially included in the China-Pakistan Economic Corridor under the Belt and Road Initiative of China. A detailed design and feasibility study was completed in October 2017, and planning was under way in November 2017.

Karachi–Lahore–Peshawar Rail Line (Expansion and Restoration)

Funders: China: None; Pakistan: None

Total Reported Cost: US$8.2 billion

Begin Date: N/A

End Date: 2022

Contractors: N/A

Description: The project is intended to rehabilitate and improve existing ML-1 railway connecting Karachi, Lahore, and Peshawar. This project will be implemented in two phases, the railway track from Karachi to Peshawar will be doubled. This project is part of China-Pakistan Economic Corridor.

Gwadar Port East Bay Expressway (Construction)

Funders: China: US$130 million; Pakistan: None; China: None

Total Reported Cost: US$159 million

Begin Date: November 2017

End Date: 2020

Contractors: China Communications Construction Company

Description: The project will link Gwadar Port with the Makran Coastal Highway in Balochistan, which will improve the logistics of transportation of imports and exports. It is part of the China-Pakistan Economic Corridor, which is a part of China's Belt and Road Initiative. China offered an interest-free loan of US$130 million for the project in September 2015, and the groundbreaking ceremony was in November 2017.

Gwadar Port Breakwater (Construction)

Funders: China: None USD

Total Reported Cost: US$123 million

Begin Date: N/A

End Date: N/A

Contractors: N/A

Description: This project is part of a larger series of construction projects on Gwadar Deep-Sea Port, the flagship project of the China-Pakistan Economic Corridor.

Gwadar Port (Freshwater Treatment and Supply)

Funders: N/A

Total Reported Cost: US$114 million

Begin Date: N/A

End Date: N/A

Contractors: N/A

Description: N/A

Gwadar Port Dredging of Berthing Areas and Channels (Construction)

Funders: N/A

Total Reported Cost: US$27 million

Begin Date: N/A

End Date: 2017

Contractors: N/A

Description: This project is part of a larger series of construction projects on Gwadar Deep-Sea Port, the flagship project of the China-Pakistan Economic Corridor. It aims to construct additional terminals and facilitate shipments. This project is financed through a Chinese Government Concession Loan (CGCC).

Gwadar Port (Infrastructure for Free Zone and EPZs Port-Related Industries)

Funders: N/A

Total Reported Cost: US$35 million

Begin Date: N/A

End Date: 2018

Contractors: N/A

Description: N/A

Gwadar–Turbat–Hoshab Section (200 km)

Funders: Pakistan National Highway Authority (NHA): PKR$14,358,400,000

Total Reported Cost: PKR$14.4 billion

Begin Date: N/A

End Date: February 4, 2016

Contractors: Frontier Works Organization (FWO)

Description: The M-8 highway is part of the China-Pakistan Economic Corridor that would connect the central, western, and eastern routes of CPEC with the Gwadar Port.

Hakla–Dera Ismail Khan Motorway (Construction)

Funders: Pakistan: US$94.4 million; China: None

Total Reported Cost: US$1.2 billion

Begin Date: N/A

End Date: 2018

Contractors: Limak Holding A.S.; Zahir Khan & Brothers (ZKB)

Description: This project consists of five sections, which are as follows: Yarik/DI Khan (on N-55) to Rehamani Khel (55 km), Rehamani Khel via Kundal to Daud Khel (70 km), Daud Khel to Tarap (50 km), Tarap to Pindigheb (50 km), and Pindigheb to Hakla on M-1 (60 km). The government of Pakistan committed financing to this project in November 2017, and the groundbreaking ceremony was held in May 2016. This project is being developed under the Belt and Road Initiative China-Pakistan Economic Corridor (CPEC) framework. This project is being constructed as part of the Western Alignment of CPEC.

National Trade Corridor Highway Tranche 2

Funders: Asian Development Bank (ADB): US$117.6 million; Pakistan: US$38 million; Department for International Development of the United Kingdom: US$82.4 million

Total Reported Cost: US$238 million

Begin Date: N/A

End Date: June 30, 2017

Contractors: JV China Gezhouba Group Co., Ltd./Ameer Muhammad Associates

Description: The project aims to develop the Hasanabdal–Havellian Expressway and link northern Pakistan to the existing expressway network. It is intended to provide better connectivity within the country and to central Asia. As of August 2017, the construction was in progress and to be completed by the end of the year.

Havelian Dry Port (Construction)

Funders: China: None USD

Total Reported Cost: US$65 million

Begin Date: N/A

End Date: N/A

Contractors: N/A

Description: The Havelian Dry Port is being constructed in the anticipated demand of future freight traffic resulting from the China-Pakistan Economic Corridor. A request for Chinese financing was submitted in November 2016, and the feasibility study was completed in June 2017. This project is part of the China-Pakistan Economic Corridor and the Belt and Road Initiative.

Havelian–Thakot Karakoram Highway Phase II (Construction)

Funders: China: None USD; Export-Import Bank of China

Total Reported Cost: US$1.3 billion

Begin Date: September 2016

End Date: December 2019

Contractors: China Communications Construction Company; China Road and Bridge Corporation

Description: The Thakot-Havelian section (73 miles/118 km) of the Karakoram Highway is currently under construction. Pakistan Prime Minister Muhammad Nawaz Sharif participated in the groundbreaking ceremony of the highway on April 28, 2016.

China–Pakistan Economic Corridor Hoshab–Basima– Sorab Highway (Upgrade and Construction)

Funders: Pakistan National Highway Authority (NHA): PKR$22,412,000,000

Total Reported Cost: PKR$22.4 billion

Begin Date: September 2007

End Date: December 2016

Contractors: Frontier Works Organization (FWO)

Description: The N-85, completed in December 2016, will serve as an important link between the cities of Quetta and Gwadar.

CPEC Karachi–Hyderabad Motorway (Upgrade)

Funders: N/A

Total Reported Cost: PKR$36 billion

Begin Date: N/A

End Date: 2018

Contractors: Frontier Works Organization (FWO): Pakistan National Highway Authority (NHA)

Description: M9 is a four-line highway and the first phase of the Lahore–Karachi Motorway that connects the cities of Hyderabad and Karachi. This improvement project, under CPEC, plans to convert the highway into a six-lane motorway.

Karachi–Lahore Motorway

Funders: China: None USD

Total Reported Cost: PKR$700 billion

Begin Date: N/A

End Date: 2018

Contractors: China Railway No. 20 Bureau Group Co., Ltd.; China State Construction Engineering Corporation (CSCEC); Zahir Khan & Brothers Engineers & Constructors

Description: The Karachi–Lahore Motorway is a 716-mile (1,152-km)-long six-lane, high-speed, controlled-access motorway currently under construction in Pakistan. Upon completion, it will connect Karachi and Lahore, and by extension Islamabad and Peshawar. The highway will also connect a number of major cities like Hyderabad, Faisalabad, and Multan. Although first devised in the early 1990s as a combination of the M3, M4, M5, M6, and M9 motorways, this project is now considered a major component of the China-Pakistan Economic Corridor.

Khuzdar–Basima Road (Construction)

Funders: China: None

Total Reported Cost: US$80 million

Begin Date: N/A

End Date: N/A

Contractors: N/A

Description: The 68-mile (110-km)-long road project includes objectives such as the road contributing to the economic and social development of Balochistan, serving mineral-rich Sandak and Rekodek areas, and linking the Highways N-85, N-25, and Motorway M-8.

M8 Package 1—Khuzdar to Kori

Funders: Pakistan National Highway Authority (NHA): None USD

Total Reported Cost: N/A

Begin Date: N/A

End Date: N/A

Contractors: Frontier Works Organization (FWO)

Description: The M-8 is a strategically important motorway being constructed in Pakistan that will connect the eastern, western, and central alignments of the China-Pakistan Economic Corridor. Its total length from Gwadar to Ratodero is 554 miles (892 km), out of which 40 miles (64 km) is in Sindh, while 514 miles (828 km) will be in Balochistan. This particular segment of the CPEC connects Khuzdar to Kori and has been completed.

M8 Package 2—Quba Saeed Khan to Ratodero

Funders: Pakistan National Highway Authority (NHA): None USD

Total Reported Cost: N/A

Begin Date: N/A

End Date: N/A

Contractors: N/A

Description: N/A

M8 Package 3—Khori to Wangu (51.08 km)

Funders: Pakistan National Highway Authority (NHA): PKR$1,116,000,000

Total Reported Cost: PKR$1.1 billion

Begin Date: October 2004

End Date: 2018

Contractors: Frontier Works Organization (FWO)

Description: The M-8 is a strategically important motorway being constructed in Pakistan that will connect the eastern, western, and central alignments of the China-Pakistan Economic Corridor. Its total length from Gwadar to Ratodero is 554 miles (892 km), out of which 40 miles (64 km) is in Sindh while 514 miles (828 km) will be in Balochistan. This part of the M-8 is currently under construction.

Wangu–Quba Saeeb Khan Road (Construction)

Funders: Pakistan National Highway Authority (NHA): PKR$525,000,000

Total Reported Cost: PKR$525 million

Begin Date: April 2004

End Date: June 2017

Contractors: Sardar Mohammad Ashraf D. Baluch (Pvt) Limited (SMADB)

Description: The M-8 is a strategically important motorway being constructed in Pakistan that will connect the eastern, western, and central alignments of the China-Pakistan Economic Corridor. Its total length from Gwadar to Ratodero is 554 miles (892 km) out of which 40 miles (64 km) is in Sindh while 514 miles (828 km) will be in Balochistan. This part of the M-8 is currently under construction.

Quba Saeed Khan–Shahdad Kot Road

Funders: Pakistan National Highway Authority (NHA): PKR$3,056,000,000

Total Reported Cost: PKR$3.1 billion

Begin Date: N/A

End Date: December 2016

Contractors: Frontier Works Organization (FWO)

Description: N/A

Mirpur–Muzaffarabad–Mansehra Road (Construction)

Funders: China: PKR$264 billion; Pakistan: None

Total Reported Cost: US$2.5 billion

Begin Date: N/A

End Date: N/A

Contractors: N/A

Description: This China-funded road project in Pakistan will stretch across 124 miles (200 km). Upon completion, it will be the shortest route from central Punjab to CPEC, through AJK, shortening the existing route by 31 miles (50 km) and saving around four to six hours of travel time.

M4 Gojra–Shorkot Motorway

Funders: Asian Development Bank (ADB): US$178 million; Pakistan: US$47 million; Department for International Development of the United Kingdom: GBP$58,850,000

Total Reported Cost: N/A

Begin Date: N/A

End Date: May 31, 2020

Contractors: China Railway First Group Co., Ltd.; Xianjiang Beixin Road & Bridge Group Co., Ltd.

Description: This project is one section of Pakistan's M4 National Motorway, from Gojra to Shorkot in Pakistan's Punjab Province. Additional financing was added to this project for the construction of the last section of road in the M4, from Shorkot to Khanewal. This project, with the additional financing and associated construction, will be a continuous road that connects Gojra, Shorkot, and Khanewal. This connection will improve the speed and safety of transport between Multan and Islamabad, and help facilitate regional trade from central Asia to the seaports of Gwadar and Karachi.

Naukundi–Mashkhel–Panjgur Road (Construction)

Funders: China: None; Pakistan: None

Total Reported Cost: US$188 million

Begin Date: N/A

End Date: N/A

Contractors: N/A

Description: This project will connect National Highway N-40 with CPEC Route N-85 and Zhob to Kuchlak, which is part of the Western Corridor CPEC Phase-II project. The Pakistani government decided to include this project in CPEC in September 2017, and as of November 2017, a pre-feasibility study of the project was completed and a detailed design was in progress.

Orange Line Metro Train Project

Funders: The Export-Import Bank of China: US$1.55 billion; Industrial and Commercial Bank of China: US$20 million

Total Reported Cost: N/A

Begin Date: 2015

End Date: 2019

Contractors: China Railway Corporation; China North Industries Corporation

Description: This is an automated light rail rapid-transit system under construction in Lahore, Punjab, Pakistan. The Orange Line is the first of the three light rail lines proposed for the Lahore Metro. When operational in 2018, it will become Pakistan's first light rail line. It will span 17 miles (27.1 km) with 16 miles (25.4 km) elevated and 1 mile (1.72) km underground.

Peshawar–Karachi Motorway Multan–Sukkur Section (Construction)

Funders: China: None USD

Total Reported Cost: US$2.8 billion

Begin Date: May 2016

End Date: May 2019

Contractors: China State Construction Engineering Corporation (CSCEC)

Description: Karachi–Peshawar Motorway project is intended to construct a six-lane motorway connecting Karachi through M-9 to Hyderabad. The intended length of the highway will be 244 miles (392 km) and planned for completion in a period of three years.

Spezand–Sariab–Kuchlak, Quetta Rail (Construction)

Funders: Pakistan: None; China: None

Total Reported Cost: US$687 million

Begin Date: N/A

End Date: N/A

Contractors: China Communications Construction Company; China Harbor Engineering Company

Description: This project is a railway line intended to serve Quetta, Balochistan, which will be single-track from Spezand to Sariab and double-track from Sariab to Kuchlak. It is part of the China-Pakistan Economic Corridor (CPEC)'s western route. Phase one of the Quetta Mass Transit system, a 30-mile (48.5-km) railroad, will be completed by 2019. The original feasibility report for phase one was submitted and reviewed by provincial authorities and Chinese officials in November 2016, and in November 2017, it was announced that the project will secure funding from a Chinese bank. The first phase (30 miles/48.5 km) will be completed by 2019 at a cost of US$214 million. This project will be developed under the China-Pakistan Economic Corridor (CPEC) framework.

Raikot–Khunjerab Karakoram Highway (Upgrade)

Funders: Export-Import Bank of China: None; Pakistan: None

Total Reported Cost: US$491 million

Begin Date: N/A

End Date: November 30, 2013

Contractors: China Road and Bridge Corporation

Description: This project, which upgraded a section of the Karakoram Highway (KKH) between Kunjerab and Raikot, is part of the China-Pakistan Economic Corridor (CPEC). The project has been controversial for its proximity to disputed territory with India.

Thakot–Raikot Karakoram Highway (Upgrade)

Funders: N/A

Total Reported Cost: PKR$8 billion

Begin Date: N/A

End Date: December 2016

Contractors: China Railway No. 17 Bureau Group Co., Ltd.

Description: The section of the Karakoram Highway from Thakot to Raikot is a 175-mile (281-km)-long stretch envisioned as a two-lane highway. The stretch falls along the new alignment of the Karakoram Highway that falls along four dams planned by the Pakistan's Water and Power Development Authority (WAPDA). In December 2017, construction was suspended due to allegations of corruption.

Yarik–Zhob Road (Upgrade)

Funders: China: None

Total Reported Cost: US$195 million

Begin Date: N/A

End Date: 2020

Contractors: N/A

Description: The project focuses on the western alignment of the China-Pakistan Economic Corridor (CPEC).

Zhob–Kuchlak Road

Funders: N/A

Total Reported Cost: US$188 million

Begin Date: N/A

End Date: N/A

Contractors: N/A

Description: N/A

Zhob–Mughalkot Road (Rehabilitation)

Funders: Pakistan: None; China: None; Asian Development Bank (ADB): None

Total Reported Cost: US$85 million

Begin Date: 2016

End Date: 2018

Contractors: N/A

Description: Construction, which was started in December 2016, was in full swing as of November 2017, and was to be completed by December 2018. The rehabilitation of this road is being conducted under the Belt and Road Initiative's China-Pakistan Economic Corridor (CPEC) framework.

QATAR

East–West Corridor

Funders: None listed: QAR$2.23 billion

Total Reported Cost: N/A

Begin Date: 2014

End Date: 2017

Contractors: China Harbor Engineering Company; Joannou & Paraskevaides (Overseas)

Description: The East–West Corridor will consist of 13.6 miles (22 km) of new road that runs five lanes in each direction. It is slated to stretch from west of Barwa City to south of Air Force Roundabout on Al Matar Street (Airport Road).

New Doha Port Navy Wharf Project

Funders: None Listed: US$170 million

Total Reported Cost: US$170 million

Begin Date: 2014

End Date: N/A

Contractors: China Communications Construction Co., Ltd.

Description: CHEC won the bid for Qatar Newport Navy Wharf Project. The project client is Qatar Newport Administrative Committee; the contract amount is about US$170 million, and the contract period is 572 days.

RUSSIA

Nizhneleninskoye–Tongjiang Rail Bridge (Construction)

See China

Moscow–Kazan High-Speed Railway

Funders: China Railway International Group: RUB$400 billion

Total Reported Cost: US$21.4 billion

Begin Date: N/A

End Date: 2022

Contractors: N/A

Description: The Moscow–Kazan High-Speed Railway will connect the Russian capital to Kazan, the capital of the Republic of Tatarstan, passing through Vladimir, Nizhny Novgorod, and Cheboksary. It plans to reach speeds up to 249 miles (400 km) per hour, and will cut traveling time from 14 hours 7 minutes down to 3 hours 30 minutes. The Moscow–Kazan section may later be extended to China, via Kazakhstan. The average annual passenger traffic is estimated at 195 million people. The Moscow–Kazan High-Speed Railway's total length will stand at around 478 miles (770 km).

Zarubino Port Construction

Funders: Summa Group: US$1.2 billion

Total Reported Cost: US$3 billion

Begin Date: N/A

End Date: 2018

Contractors: China Merchants Holding International Company, Ltd.; Summa Group

Description: To accommodate transit of Chinese goods between the northeastern and southern provinces of China, Russia's Summa Group is cooperating with China Merchants Holding International to build a deep-water port 50 miles (80 km) from Vladivostok at Zarubino.

SAUDI ARABIA

Abu Bakar Intersection Bridge

Funders: N/A

Total Reported Cost: N/A

Begin Date: N/A

End Date: N/A

Contractors: China Civil Engineering Construction Corporation

Description: China Civil is constructing a bridge at the intersection of Arafat Road with Abu Baker.

Bridge at Arafat Road and Al-Kharj Road in Riyadh

Funders: N/A

Total Reported Cost: N/A

Begin Date: N/A

End Date: N/A

Contractors: China Civil Engineering Construction Corporation

Description: China Civil is constructing a bridge at the intersection of Arafat Road with Al-Kharj Road in Riyadh (BIAK for short).

Civil and Track Works Contract CTW400

Funders: N/A

Total Reported Cost: N/A

Begin Date: December 10, 2009

End Date: 2009

Contractors: China Civil Engineering Construction Corporation

Description: China Civil Engineering Construction Corporation (CCECC), one of China's major construction firms, is currently involved in the Civil and Track Works Contract CTW400, from Az Zabirah Junction to King Khalid International Airport.

Dammam Riyadh Freight Line Phase 2

Funders: N/A

Total Reported Cost: SAR$160 million

Begin Date: 2015

End Date: February 2017

Contractors: China Railway Construction Corporation

Description: Saudi Railways Organization awarded China Railway Construction Corp. (CRCC) a SAR$160 million contract to undertake the 57-mile (91-km) second phase of upgrading the Dammam–Riyadh freight line. The specifications for the 23-month project is to increase capacity includes raising the maximum axle load to 32.5 tonnes.

Hamza Intersection Bridge

Funders: N/A

Total Reported Cost: N/A

Begin Date: N/A

End Date: N/A

Contractors: China Civil Engineering Construction Corporation

Description: China Civil is constructing a bridge at Hamza intersection in Najran.

Medina–Mecca (Makkah) High-Speed Rail Construction

Funders: N/A

Total Reported Cost: EUR$10 billion

Begin Date: March 2009

End Date: September 25, 2018

Contractors: Al Arrab Contracting; Al Rosan Company for Contracting; Al Shoula Group; Bouygues Group; Buro Happold Engineering; China Railway Engineering Corporation (CRECG); Foster + Partners; Imathia Construction; Ineco; Mada Group for Industrial and Commercial Investment; Obrascon Huarte Lain, S.A. (OHL); Saudi Binladin Group; Saudi Oger Ltd.; Administrador de Infraestructuras Ferroviarias (ADIF); S. A. de Obras y Servicios, COPASA

Description: The Haramain High-Speed Rail connects Medina (Al Madi-
nah Al-Munawara) in the north to Mecca (Makkah) in the south. One
of the main objectives for the railway is to carry Hajj pilgrims, reliev-
ing traffic on highways between the two cities. It will also connect to
King Abdulaziz International Airport and Jeddah.

Prince Muteb Intersection Bridge in Najran

Funders: N/A

Total Reported Cost: N/A

Begin Date: N/A

End Date: N/A

Contractors: China Civil Engineering Construction Corporation

Description: China Civil is constructing a bridge at the Prince Muteb Intersection in Najran.

King Abdulaziz Intersection Tunnel

Funders: N/A

Total Reported Cost: N/A

Begin Date: N/A

End Date: N/A

Contractors: China Civil Engineering Construction Corporation

Description: China Civil, an engineering construction corporation from
China, is currently involved in the construction of a tunnel at the inter-
section of King Abdulaziz Road with Palestine Street and Al Hamra
Street in Jeddah (KAAT).

SERBIA

Belgrade Bypass

Funders: N/A

Total Reported Cost: EUR$207 million

Begin Date: N/A

End Date: N/A

Contractors: Power Construction Corporation of China

Description: N/A

Budapest–Belgrade High-Speed Railway—Serbian Section (Construction)

Funders: Export-Import Bank of China: US$297,600,000

Total Reported Cost: N/A

Begin Date: 2017

End Date: 2020

Contractors: N/A

Description: This Chinese-backed high-speed railway is intended to link the capitals of Hungary and Serbia and has been celebrated as a flagship project under China's "16 + 1" format and Belt and Road Initiative.

Corridor XI motorway (Obrenovac–Ub and Lajkovac–Ljig sections)

Funders: Export-Import Bank of China: US$301,000,000; Serbia: US$32,740,000

Total Reported Cost: US$334 million

Begin Date: N/A

End Date: 2017

Contractors: Shandong Hi-Speed Group

Description: N/A

Stublenica Industrial, Commercial, and Technology Park

Funders: China Development Bank: None USD

Total Reported Cost: EUR$1.2 billion

Begin Date: N/A

End Date: N/A

Contractors: N/A

Description: Construction of the industrial, commercial, and technology park Stublenica.

SLOVAKIA

Kosice–Vienna Railway (Construction)

See Austria

SRI LANKA

Central Expressway E04, Kadawatha–Mirigama Section (Construction)

Funders: Mitsubishi UFJ Financial Group: None USD; Exim Bank of India: None USD

Total Reported Cost: N/A

Begin Date: N/A

End Date: 2020

Contractors: N/A

Description: This is the first section of the E04 Central Expressway project in Sri Lanka, which will connect Colombo to Kandy. This section entails the road construction between Kadawatha and Mirigama.

Hambantota Deep-Sea Port Phase 1 (PPP)

Funders: China National Electric Import & Export Corporation (CUEC): US$307 million; Sri Lanka Ministry of Transport and Civil Aviation: US$54,176,470

Total Reported Cost: US$505 million

Begin Date: January 15, 2008

End Date: November 18, 2010

Contractors: China Harbor Engineering Company; Sino-German Bausparkasse Co., Ltd.

Description: This project is for the construction of a deep-sea port in southeastern Sri Lanka's Southern Province. Currently, construction is between phases II and III, although widespread public anger persists over the financing agreement between the Sri Lankan government and Chinese funders. In December 2016, the Sri Lankan government announced that it would sell an 80 percent stake in the Hambantota Port to China Merchants Port Holding Co. for $1.12 billion. This announcement triggered protests by trade unions and opposition groups causing the two parties to revise China's stake in the joint venture to 70 percent. The concession agreement was completed on July 29, 2017, and in December 2017, Sri Lanka formally handed over port operations to China Merchants Port Holding. Almost directly across India lies the Gwadar Port, a $46 billion project that is a cornerstone for the China-Pakistan Economic Corridor (CPEC).

Hambantota Deep-Sea Port Phase II (PPP)

Funders: Export-Import Bank of China: US$158,350,000; Export-Import Bank of China: US$600 million; Export-Import Bank of China: US$51 million

Total Reported Cost: US$809.4 million

Begin Date: November 25, 2012

End Date: July 15, 2015

Contractors: China Communications Construction Company; China Harbor Engineering Company

Description: Funding for the port was split into three types of loans, all financed by Chinese companies. The port failed to attract the needed traffic to pay back high government debt to China and in late December 2016, President Maithripala Sirisena announced that the port would lease 80 percent ownership of the port-operating companies to China Merchants Holding for $1.12 billion over 99 years. This announcement triggered protests by trade unions and opposition groups causing the two parties to revise China's stake in the joint venture to 70 percent. The concession agreement was completed on July 29, 2017, and in December 2017, Sri Lanka formally handed over port operations to China Merchants Port Holding.

Matara–Kataragama Railway Phase 1 (Extension)

Funders: Export-Import Bank of China: None USD

Total Reported Cost: US$1 billion

Begin Date: 2013

End Date: 2020

Contractors: China Railway No. 5 Engineering Group; China Machinery Corporation; China National Machinery Imp. & Exp. Corp.

Description: Phase 1 of the project is intended to modernize and extend the railroad from Matara to Beliatta. It aims to improve the quality of railway connection in the southern Sri Lanka.

TAJIKISTAN

Khojend–Isfara Highway (Rehabilitation)

Funders: Tajikistan: US$9,000,000; International Development Association (IDA) (World Bank): US$38,250,000; International Development Association (IDA) (World Bank): US$6,750,000

Total Reported Cost: US$54 million

Begin Date: 2016

End Date: August 31, 2020

Contractors: China Railway Group

Description: This project aims to increase transport connectivity between the Republic of Tajikistan and neighboring countries and to support improvements in road operations and asset-management practices. The road sections to be financed under CARs-2 prioritize connectivity between Sugd Oblast in Tajikistan with Batken and Osh Oblasts in the Kyrgyz Republic and Ferghana Oblast in Uzbekistan.

Silk Road Economic Belt Railway, Tajikistan Section

Funders: N/A

Total Reported Cost: N/A

Begin Date: N/A

End Date: N/A

Contractors: N/A

Description: N/A

THAILAND

Sino–Thai High-Speed Rail (Phase 1), Section Bangkok–Nakhon Ratchasima

Funders: N/A

Total Reported Cost: THB$179 billion

Begin Date: December 21, 2017

End Date: 2021

Contractors: Thailand Department of Highways

Description: Following a delayed start due to the extension of negotiations, Prime Minister Prayut Chan-o-cha involved Article 44 of the Thai Constitution, giving him absolute power to sign the inaugural contracts for the Bangkok–Nakhon Ratchasima section of the Sino–Thai High-Speed Rail's first phase in September 2017.

Sino–Thai High-Speed Rail (Phase 1), Section Nakhon Ratchasima–Nong Khai

Funders: N/A

Total Reported Cost: N/A

Begin Date: N/A

End Date: N/A

Contractors: N/A

Description: N/A

Sino–Thai High Speed Rail (Phase 2), Section Kaeng Khoi–Map Ta Phut

Funders: N/A

Total Reported Cost: N/A

Begin Date: N/A

End Date: N/A

Contractors: N/A

Description: N/A

TURKEY
Edirne–Sofia High-Speed Rail (Construction)

See Bulgaria

TURKMENISTAN
Silk Road Economic Belt Railway, Turkmenistan Section

Funders: N/A
Total Reported Cost: N/A
Begin Date: N/A
End Date: N/A
Contractors: N/A
Description: N/A

UNITED ARAB EMIRATES
Khalifa Port Container Terminal 2

Funders: N/A
Total Reported Cost: US$738 million
Begin Date: N/A
End Date: 2018
Contractors: COSCO Pacific
Description: N/A

UZBEKISTAN
Angren–Pap Railway (Construction)

Funders: Uzbekistan: US$1,088,750,000; Export-Import Bank of China: US$350 million; International Bank for Reconstruction and Development (IBRD) (World Bank): US$195 million

Total Reported Cost: US$1.6 billion
Begin Date: N/A

End Date: 2016

Contractors: Belam-Riga SIA; China Railway Tunnel Group; Chkz-Export; JSC Yujnouralskiy Armaturno-Izolyatorniy Zavod; Jiangsu Zhongtian Technology Co., Ltd.; Lepstroy; O'zelektroapparat-Electroshield OJSC (JV); Pinggao Group Co., Ltd.; Rostok Cis K/S; Shanghai Electric Power Transmission & Distribution Engineering Co., Ltd.; Société des Anciens Etablissements L. Geismar; Uralspecmash-Export; JSC Uzbekistan Railways (Uzbek Temir Yollari); Uzelectroapparat

Description: This railway improves connectivity with Uzbekistan's Fergana Valley and allows freight traffic to bypass neighboring Tajikistan. The Qamchiq Tunnel, an important part of the Angren–Pap railway line, is the longest tunnel in central Asia and was constructed by a Chinese company, China Railway Tunnel Group.

Silk Road Economic Belt Railway, Uzbekistan Section

Funders: The World Bank: None USD; Islamic Development Bank: None USD; European Bank for Reconstruction and Development (EBRD): None USD

Total Reported Cost: N/A

Begin Date: N/A

End Date: N/A

Contractors: N/A

Description: N/A

Notes

CHAPTER 1

1. Sydney Freedberg Jr., "Pentagon to Retire USS Truman Early, Shrinking Carrier Fleet to 10," Breaking Defense, February 27, 2019, https://breakingdefense.com/2019/02/pentagon-to-retire-uss-truman-early-shrinking-carrier-fleet-to-10.

2. Irene Yuan Sun, *The Next Factory of the World: How Chinese Investment Is Reshaping Africa* (Boston: Harvard Business Review Press, 2017), 42.

CHAPTER 2

1. Benjamin Habib and Viktor Faulknor, "The Belt and Road Initiative: China's Vision for Globalisation, Beijing-Style," The Conversation, May 16, 2017, theconversation.com/the-belt-and-road-initiative-chinas-vision-for-globalisation-beijing-style-77705.

2. Jonathan E. Hillman, "How Big Is China's Belt and Road?" Center for Strategic and International Studies, April 3, 2018, www.csis.org/analysis/how-big-chinas-belt-and-road; "Chinese Firm To Build Cars For Metro Subway, Rail Lines," CBS Broadcasting Inc., March 23, 2017, losangeles.cbslocal.com/2017/03/23/chinese-firm-to-build-cars-for-metro-subway-rail-lines.

3. Robert R. Gilruth, "I Believe We Should Go to the Moon," NASA, history.nasa.gov/SP-350/ch-2-1.html.

4. Association of Southeast Asian Nations, asean.org.

5. Kishore Mahbubani, *The New Asian Hemisphere: The Irresistible Shift of Global Power to the East* (New York, Public Affairs, 2008).

6. "Approved Projects," Asian Infrastructure Investment Bank, www.aiib.org/en/projects/approved/index.html.

7. www.ft.com/content/762ce968-bcee-11e5-a8c6-deeeb63d6d4b.

8. www.ft.com/content/da2258f6-2752-11e8-b27e-cc62a39d57a0.

9. http://www.chinabankingnews.com/2017/09/21/chinas-belt-road-initia tive-credit-positive-participants-says-moodys/.

10. https://www.citibank.com/icg/sa/public_sector/Public_Sector_Perspec tives_2017_2018/files/assets/basic-html/page-14.html.

11. HSBC Insights, "China's Belt and Road Gains Momentum," March 8, 2018, www.gbm.hsbc.com/insights/growth/china-belt-and-road-gains-mo mentum?pid=HBEU:mi:IS:XX:HOM:1803:001:ChinaBRIMomentum.

12. Ibid.

13. http://alliance-us.org.

14. P. K. Balachandran, "China-Funded Confucius Institutes Change Goals to Suit Local Needs," Opinion Pages, July 1, 2018, opinion.bdnews24 .com/2018/07/01/china-funded-confucius-institutes-change-goals-to-suit -local-needs.

15. Melissa Korn and O'Keeffe, Kate, "Chinese Programs in U.S. Challenged," *The Wall Street Journal,* February 28, 2019.

16. Jagannath P. Panda, "What the Inclusion of BRI in the Chinese Constitution Implies," Institute for Defense Studies and Analyses, November 7, 2017, idsa.in/idsacomments/what-the-inclusion-of-bri-in-the-chinese-consti tution-implies_jpanda_071117.

CHAPTER 3

1. European Central Bank, "Use of the Euro," www.ecb.europa.eu/euro /intro/html/index.en.html.

2. Jennifer L. Goss, "The Marshall Plan," ThoughtCo., February 19, 2019, www.thoughtco.com/marshall-plan-economic-aid-1779313.

3. Detroit Historical Society, "Arsenal of Democracy," detroithistorical .org/learn/encyclopedia-of-detroit/arsenal-democracy.

4. *Transatlantic Economy 2018,* American Chamber of Commerce to the European Union, March 7, 2018, www.amchameu.eu/publications/tran satlantic-economy-2018.

5. "Chinese Economic Power Will Dominate the 21st Century," *The National,* October 23, 2017, www.thenational.ae/world/asia/chinese-eco nomic-power-will-dominate-the-21st-century-1.669759.

6. Ash Carter, "Remarks by Secretary Carter and Q&A at the Shangri-La Dialogue, Singapore," U.S. Department of Defense, June 5, 2016, www .defense.gov/News/Transcripts/Transcript-View/Article/791472/remarks -by-secretary-carter-and-qa-at-the-shangri-la-dialogue-singapore.

7. Ibid.

8. Jacob Wolinsky, "Trump's Plans To Further Slap Tariffs Are Woefully Misguided: Dr. Parag Khanna," Value Walk, October 29, 2018, www.valuewalk.com/2018/10/1-trading-partner-china.

9. Oliver Holmes, "What Is the US Military's Presence Near North Korea?" *The Guardian*, August 9, 2017, www.theguardian.com/us-news/2017/aug/09/what-is-the-us-militarys-presence-in-south-east-asia.

10. RAND Corporation, Report MR1244 "China's Quest for Energy Security," https://www.rand.org/search.html?query=mr1244.

11. "The Explainer: China's Malacca Dilemma," BJ's nocabbages (blog), November 14, 2012, www.bjnocabbages.com/2012/11/the-explainer-chinas-malacca-dilemma.html.

12. "What Is the Malacca Dilemma?" www.quora.com/What-is-the-Malacca-Dilemma.

13. Robert D. Kaplan, "The South China Sea Will Be the Battleground of the Future," *Business Insider*, February 6, 2016, www.businessinsider.com/why-the-south-china-sea-is-so-crucial-2015-2.

14. "Advance Policy Questions for Admiral Philip Davidson, USN Expected Nominee for Commander, U.S. Pacific Command," Department of Defense Reforms, www.armed-services.senate.gov/imo/media/doc/Davidson_APQs_04-17-18.pdf.

15. "Carrier Strike Group," U.S. Navy, www.public.navy.mil/airfor/cvn69/Pages/CARRIER%20STRIKE%20GROUP.aspx.

16. Jerry Hendrix, "At What Cost a Carrier?" Center for a New American Security, March 11, 2013, www.cnas.org/publications/reports/at-what-cost-a-carrier.

17. Ibid.

18. *Military and Security Developments Involving the People's Republic of China 2018, Annual Report to Congress,* Office of the Secretary of Defense, 2017, media.defense.gov/2018/Aug/16/2001955282/-1/-1/1/2018-CHINA-MILITARY-POWER-REPORT.PDF.

19. Ibid.

CHAPTER 4

1. Reconnecting Asia, reconnectingasia.csis.org.

2. Center for Strategic and International Studies, csis.org.

3. Estimates of the final Chinese investment in CPEC run as high as $67 billion, but as of October 31, 2018, the CPEC projects approved by the Chinese and Pakistani governments amounted to $45 billion.

4. Shayan Rauf, "China-Pakistan Economic Corridor (CPEC)," www
.britannica.com/topic/China-Pakistan-Economic-Corridor.

5. Ibid.

6. "About Deloitte," www2.deloitte.com/pk/en/pages/about-deloitte
/articles/about-deloitte.html.

7. Ibid.

8. Dr. Ishrat Husain, *CPEC & Pakistani Economy: An Appraisal,* and
CPEC & Pakistan's Economy: A Way Forward (Islamabad, Pakistan: Center of Excellence for CPEC, 2017).

9. Ibid.

10. Ibid.

11. Robert Ayres and Benjamin Warr, *The Economic Growth Engine:
How Energy and Work Drive Material Prosperity* (The International Institute
for Applied Systems Analysis), https://www.e-elgar.com/shop/the-economic
-growth-engine?___website=uk_warehouse.

12. *The Economist,* August 4, 2018, 33.

13. Ferdinand Bada, "Where Is the Strait of Hormuz?" *World Atlas*,
January 18, 2018.

14. Anatol Lieven, *Pakistan: A Hard Country* (New York: Public Affairs,
2011), 343.

15. Ibid., 344.

16. Adnan Aamir, "Terrorist Attacks Show Pakistan's Need to Reassure
China on Security," *Nikkei Asian Review*, August 21, 2018, asia.nikkei.com
/Spotlight/Belt-and-Road/Terrorist-attacks-show-Pakistan-s-need-to
-reassure-China-on-security.

17. "Gwadar Uplift under CPEC to Benefit Balochistan," Xinhua, September 2, 1018, www.thenews.com.pk/print/359864-gwadar-uplift-under
-cpec-to-benefit-balochistan.

18. George Magnus, *Red Flags, Why Xi's China Is in Jeopardy* (New
Haven and London: Yale University Press, 2018), 180–81.

19. Anwar Iqbal, "Chinese Investments Dwarf American Package: US
Media," *Dawn*, April 21, 2015, www.dawn.com/news/1177244.

20. Richard Sisk, "Pakistan Likely to Keep Open Supply Routes to
Afghanistan," Military.com, January 7, 2018, www.military.com/daily
-news/2018/01/07/pakistan-likely-keep-open-supply-routes-afghanistan.html.

21. Ayaz Gul, "Pakistan Mulls NATO Offer to Ship Afghan Supplies
Through Gwadar Port," VOA News, January 10, 2018, www.voanews.com
/a/pakistan-mulls-natio-offer-to-ship-afghan-supplies-through-gwadar
-port/4201473.html.

22. Hamid Butt, "Pakistan, China Sign 15 Agreements, Mous on Bilateral Cooperation," *The Business,* November 3, 2018, thebusiness.com .pk/2018/11/03/pakistan-china-sign-15-agreements-mous-on-bilateral -cooperation.

23. Nan Lwin, "Gov't Signs MoU with Beijing to Build China-Myanmar Economic Corridor," The Irrawaddy, September 13, 2018, www.irrawaddy .com/news/burma/govt-signs-mou-beijing-build-china-myanmar-economic -corridor.html.

24. Ibid.

25. Gregory Poling, "Kyaukpyu: Connecting China to the Indian Ocean," *CSIS Briefs*, April 2, 2018.

26. Atul Aneja, "Rohingya Crisis Reinforce China-Myanmar Bonds," *The Hindu,* September 15, 2018, www.thehindu.com/news/international /rohingya-crisis-reinforce-china-myanmar-bonds/article24955917.ece.

27. Ibid.

28. Ibid.

29. David Pilling, "Pipeline marks scramble for Myanmar," *Financial Times*, January 30, 2013, www.ft.com/content/8cc53250-6a2d-11e2-a7d2 -00144feab49a.

30. Khin OO Tha, "Burmese Arrested after Dispute with Chinese Pipeline Workers," The Irrawaddy, January 31, 2014, www.irrawaddy.com/news /burma/burmese-arrested-dispute-chinese-pipeline-workers.html.

31. Giuseppe Gabusi and Simone Dossi, "Damned Be Myanmar's Myitsone Dam?" East Asia Forum, July 16, 2017, www.eastasiaforum.org/2017 /07/16/damned-be-myanmars-myitsone-dam.

32. "Myanmar Scales Back Chinese-Backed Port Project over Debt Fears," *The Guardian,* August 2, 2018, www.theguardian.com/world/2018 /aug/02/myanmar-scales-back-chinese-backed-port-project-over-debt -fears.

33. Ibid.

34. Kiran Stacey, "China Signs 99-year Lease on Sri Lanka's Hambantota Port," *Financial Times,* December 11, 2017, www.ft.com/content /e150ef0c-de37-11e7-a8a4-0a1e63a52f9c.

35. Maria Abi-Habib, "How China Got Sri Lanka to Cough Up a Port," *New York Times,* June 25, 2018, www.nytimes.com/2018/06/25/world/asia /china-sri-lanka-port.html.

36. John J. Xenakis, "World View: China Takes Control of Sri Lanka's Strategically Valuable Hambantota Seaport," Breitbart, August 6, 2017, www.breitbart.com/national-security/2017/08/06/6-aug-17-world-view

-china-takes-control-of-sri-lankas-strategically-valuable-hambantota
-seaport.

37. Maria Abi-Habib, "How China Got Sri Lanka to Cough Up a Port," *New York Times,* June 25, 2018, www.nytimes.com/2018/06/25/world/asia /china-sri-lanka-port.html.

38. "Bofors arms deal: Italian was 'paid kickbacks'," *BBC News*, January 4, 2011.

39. "Concession Agreement in Relation to Hambantota Port, Sri Lanka," www.cmport.com.hk/UpFiles/bpic/2017-07/20170725061311456.pdf.

40. Maria Abi-Habib, "How China Got Sri Lanka to Cough Up a Port," *New York Times,* June 25, 2018, www.nytimes.com/2018/06/25/world/asia /china-sri-lanka-port.html.

41. "Profile: Mahinda Rajapaksa," *BBC News*, August 18, 2015.

42. Ibid.

43. "SL Navy's Southern Command Moving to Hambantota—PM Office," *Daily Mirror,* June 30, 2018, www.dailymirror.lk/article/SL-Navy -s-Southern-Command-moving-to-Hambantota-PM-office-152049.html.

44. Rahul Singh, "India Unfazed by Sri Lankan Navy's Proposed Shift to Hambantota Port Run by Chinese," *Hindustan Times,* July 14, 2018, www .hindustantimes.com/india-news/india-unfazed-by-sri-lanka-navy-s-pro posed-shift-navy-to-hambantota-port-run-by-chinese/story-cobE5YyH EegsboyQeXf2DP.html.

45. Jason Horowitz and Liz Alderman, "Chastised by E.U., a Resentful Greece Embraces China's Cash and Interests," *New York Times,* August 26, 2017, www.nytimes.com/2017/08/26/world/europe/greece-china-piraeus -alexis-tsipras.html.

46. "The Geopolitical Significance of Piraeus Port to China," PAGEO Research Institute, March 19, 2017, www.geopolitika.hu/en/2017/03/19/the -geopolitical-significance-of-piraeus-port-to-china.

47. Keith Johnson, "In Odyssey for Chinese, Greece Sells Its Fabled Port of Piraeus," Foreign Policy, April 8, 2016, www.foreignpolicy.com/2016/04 /08/in-odyssey-for-chinese-greece-sells-its-fabled-port-of-piraeus.

48. "Greece Sells Largest Port Piraeus to Chinese Company," RT, April 8, 2016, www.rt.com/business/338949-greece-china-port-sale.

49. James T. Areddy, "Trophy Infrastructure, Troublesome Debt: China Makes Inroads in Europe," *Wall Street Journal,* November 5, 2018, www .wsj.com/articles/chinas-newest-bid-for-influence-runs-through-the-wests -backyard-1541435003.

50. Georgi Gotev, "EU Unable to Adopt Statement Upholding South China Sea Ruling," Euractiv, July 14, 2016, www.euractiv.com/section

/global-europe/news/eu-unable-to-adopt-statement-upholding-south-china
-sea-ruling.

51. Jason Horowitz and Liz Alderman, "Chastised by E.U., a Resentful Greece Embraces China's Cash and Interests," *New York Times,* August 26, 2017, www.nytimes.com/2017/08/26/world/europe/greece-china-piraeus -alexis-tsipras.html.

52. F. William Engdahl, "Will China BRI Cause East West Rupture in EU?" *New Eastern Outlook,* January 29, 2018, journal-neo.org/2018/01/29 /will-china-bri-cause-east-west-rupture-in-eu.

53. Ibid.

54. Conor Finnegan, "VP Pence Paints China as Foremost Threat to US: 'We will not be intimidated,'" *ABC News,* October 4, 2018, abcnews.go.com /US/vice-president-mike-pence-warns-china-stand/story?id=58282875.

CHAPTER 5

1. *Travel China Guide*, "Beijing Weather in September," www.travel chinaguide.com/cityguides/beijing/weather-september.htm.

2. Shannon Tiezzi, "FOCAC 2018: Rebranding China in Africa," *The Diplomat*, September 5, 2018, https://thediplomat.com/2018/09/focac-2018 -rebranding-china-in-africa/

3. Ibid.

4. Grant Harris, "By Ignoring Africa, US Cedes Jobs To China," *Forbes,* June 14, 2017, www.forbes.com/sites/realspin/2017/06/14/by-ignoring-africa -u-s-cedes-jobs-to-china/#255645777f6d.

5. Grisons Peak, "BRI Pulse; Upcoming Beijing Summit of the Forum on China-Africa Cooperation (FOCAC); The Initial Silk Road Heads West across Africa?" August 25, 2018, chinaglobalimpact.files.wordpress.com /2018/08/bri-pulse-release.pdf.

6. Irene Yuan Sun, *The Next Factory of the World: How Chinese Investment Is Reshaping Africa* (Boston: Harvard Business Review Press, 2017).

7. Ibid., 30.

8. Ibid., 6.

9. Ibid., 29.

10. Ibid., 26.

11. Ibid., 92.

12. "China's Investments in Africa: What's the Real Story," Public Policy, Knowledge @ Wharton, Jan. 19, 2016, knowledge.wharton.upenn.edu /article/chinas-investments-in-africa-whats-the-real-story.

13. Lillian Mutiso, "10 Mega Infrastructure Projects in Africa Funded by China," Moguldom, March 17, 2016, moguldom.com/121477/10-mega -infrastructural-projects-in-africa-funded-by-china/8.

14. Zineb Boujrada, "This Tiny Country Has the Most Foreign Military Bases," Culture Trip, March 16, 2018, theculturetrip.com/africa/djibouti /articles/why-does-djibouti-have-the-most-foreign-military-bases.

15. Brad Lendon and Steve George, "China Sends Troops to Djibouti, Establishes First Overseas Military Base," CNN, July 13, 2017, www.cnn .com/2017/07/12/asia/china-djibouti-military-base/index.html.

16. Central Intelligence Agency, *World Fact Book*, Djibouti, https://www .cia.gov/search?q=africa&site=CIA&output=xml_no_dtd&client=CIA &myAction=%2Fsearch&proxystylesheet=CIA&submitMethod=get.

17. BBC News, "Ethiopia-Djibouti Electric Railway Line Opens," October 2016, www.bbc.com/news/world-africa-37562177.

18. DP World, "Who We Are," February 24, 2018, www.dpworld.com /who-we-are.

19. Patrick Martin, "Could China Squeeze the U.S. Out of Its Only Permanent Military Base in Africa?" *The Washington Post,* December 14, 2018, www.washingtonpost.com/national-security/2018/12/14/could-china -squeeze-us-out-its-only-permanent-military-base-africa/?utm_term =.612454b0a5cb.

20. Ibid.

21. Edwin Mora, "China Launches 'Belt and Road' Research Center in Egypt," Breitbart, January 14, 2019, www.breitbart.com/national-security /2019/01/14/china-launches-belt-road-research-center-egypt.

22. Hisham A. B. Metwally, "BRI Chinese Investment Grabs Egypt's Attention," China Focus, September 19, 2018, www.cnfocus.com/bri-chin ese-investment-grabs-egypt-s-attention.

23. Mahmoud Fouly, "Interview: China's BRI 'Game Changer;' for World Economy: Egypt's Ex-Diplomat," *Xinhuanet,* January 1, 2019, www .xinhuanet.com/english/2019-01/25/c_137774628.htm.

24. Hisham A. B. Metwally, "BRI Chinese Investment Grabs Egypt's Attention," China Focus, September 19, 2018, www.cnfocus.com/bri -chinese-investment-grabs-egypt-s-attention.

25. Lillian Mutiso, "10 Mega Infrastructure Projects in Africa Funded by China," Moguldom, March 17, 2016, moguldom.com/121477/10-mega -infrastructural-projects-in-africa-funded-by-china/4.

26. CIA World Handbook, https://www.cia.gov/library/publications/the -world-factbook/geos/od.html.

CHAPTER 6

1. "Trade Turnover across China's 'One Belt, One Road' Exceeds $5 Trillion since 2013," *RT News,* December 23, 2018, www.rt.com/business /447240-silk-road-thousands-jobs.

2. Chun Han Wong, "Xi Jinping's Strongman Rule Comes Under Fire as China Celebrates Deng's Reforms," *The Wall Street Journal,* December 18, 2018, www.wsj.com/articles/xi-jinpings-strongman-rule-comes-under-fire -as-china-celebrates-dengs-reforms-11545047738.

3. "UBS, Deutsche Bank Calculate Growth Impact from Tariff Hikes," *Bloomberg News,* June 19, 2018, www.bloomberg.com/news/articles/2018 -06-20/trump-s-tariffs-could-deliver-a-sizable-hit-to-china-s-economy.

4. Gabriel Wildau and Tom Mitchell, "China Income Inequality among the World's Worst," *Financial Times,* January 14, 2016, www.ft.com/content /3c521faa-baa6-11e5-a7cc-280dfe875e28.

5. George Magnus, *Red Flags, Why Xi's China Is in Jeopardy* (New Haven and London: Yale University Press, 2018), 76, 77.

6. Lingling Wei, "China's Annual Economic Growth Rate Is Slowest Since 1990," *The Wall Street Journal,* January 21, 2019, www.wsj.com /articles/china-annual-economic-growth-rate-is-slowest-since-1990 -11548037761.

7. Hal Brands, *What Good Is Grand Strategy, Power and Purpose in American Statecraft from Harry S. Truman to George W. Bush* (Cornell University Press: Ithaca and London, 2014), 4.

8. Arthur Villasanta, "China to Take Over Kenya's Largest Port as Debt Repayment," *Invests,* January 2, 2019, https://www.investmentwatchblog.com /china-to-take-over-kenyas-main-port-over-huge-unpaid-chinese-loan/

9. Jennifer Bell, "Gulf States Key to World That Is Now Asia First, Says Author Parag Khanna," *Gulf News,* January 11, 2019, www.arabnews.com /node/1433196/world.

10. Michael Forsythe, "China Aims to Spend at Least 360 Billion on Renewable Energy by 2020," *The New York Times,* January 5, 2017, www .nytimes.com/2017/01/05/world/asia/china-renewable-energy-investment .html.

11. Josh Zumbrun, "World Bank President Plans Early Exit," *The Wall Street Journal,* January 7, 2019, www.wsj.com/articles/world-bank-president -jim-yong-kim-to-resign-in-february-11546879066.

12. Glenn Thrush, "Trump Embraces Foreign Aid to Counter China's Global Influence," *The New York Times,* October 14, 2018.

13. Shi Jiangtao and Owen Churchill, "US Competes with China's Belt and Road Initiative with US $113 Million Asian Investment Programme," *South China Morning Post,* August 2, 2018, www.scmp.com/news/china /economy/article/2157381/us-competes-chinas-belt-and-road-initiative -new-asian-investment.

Selected Bibliography

I list here only the resources that were used in writing this book. This bibliography is by no means a complete record of all the works and sources I have consulted. It indicates the substance and range of reading upon which I have formed my ideas, and I intend it to serve as a convenience for those who wish to pursue the subject of this book in more detail and to strike off on their own.

Allison, Graham. "The Thucydides Trap: Are the U.S. and China Headed for War?" *The Atlantic*, September 24, 2015.

Annual Report to Congress. *Military and Security Developments Involving the People's Republic of China* (Washington, DC: Office of the Secretary of Defense, 2018, 2017, 2016).

Brands, Hal. *What Good Is Grand Strategy? Power and Purpose in American Statecraft from Harry S. Truman to George W. Bush* (Ithaca and London: Cornell University Press, 2014).

Chang, Jung. *Empress Dowager Cixi: The Concubine Who Launched Modern China* (Toronto: Random House Canada, 2013).

Doig, Will. *High-Speed Empire: Chinese Expansion and the Future of Southeast Asia* (New York: Columbia Global Reports, 2018).

Fishman, Ted C. *China Inc.: How the Rise of the Next Superpower Challenges America and the World* (New York: Scribner, 2005).

Frankopan, Peter. *The Silk Roads: A New History of the World* (New York: Alfred A. Knopf, 2016).

Hotta, Eri. *Japan 1941: Countdown to Infamy* (New York: Alfred A. Knopf, 2013).

Howell, David. *Empires in Collision: The Green versus Black Struggle for Our Energy Future* (London: Gilgamesh Publishing, 2016).

Husain, Ishrat. *CPEC & Pakistan's Economy: A Way Forward* (Islamabad, Pakistan: Center of Excellence, China-Pakistan Economic Corridor, 2017).

Magnus, George. *Red Flags: Why China Is in Jeopardy* (New Haven & London: Yale University Press, 2018).

Mahbubani, Kishore. *Asia, The West, and the Logic of One World: The Great Convergence* (New York: Public Affairs, 2013).

Mahbubani, Kishore. *The New Asian Hemisphere: The Irresistible Shift of Global Power to the East* (New York: Public Affairs, 2008).

McGregor Richard. *Asia's Reckoning: China, Japan, and the Fate of U.S. Power in the Pacific Century* (New York: Viking, 2017).

Mitter, Rana. *China's War with Japan 1937–1945: The Struggle for Survival* (London: Allen Lane, 2013).

Osnos, Evan. *Age of Ambition: Chasing Fortune, Truth & Faith in the New China* (New York: Farrar, Straus and Giroux, 2015).

Pomfret, John. *The Beautiful Country and the Middle Kingdom: America and China, 1776 to the Present* (New York: Henry Holt and Company, 2016).

Posen, Barry R. *Restraint: A New Foundation for U.S. Grand Strategy* (Ithaca & London: Cornell University Press, 2014).

Shambaugh, David. *Tangled Titans: The United States and China* (Maryland USA: Rowman & Littlefield Publishers, Inc., 2013).

Sun, Irene Yuan. *The Next Factory of the World: How Chinese Investment is Reshaping Africa* (Boston, Massachusetts: Harvard University Business Press, 2018).

Vatikiotis, Michael. *Blood and Silk: Power and Conflict in Modern Southeast Asia* (Great Britain: Weidenfeld and Nicolson, 2017).

White, Hugh. *The China Choice: Why We Should Share Power* (Oxford, UK: Oxford University Press, 2014).

Yew, Lee Kuan. *One Man's View of the World* (Singapore: Straits Times Press, 2003).

Yoshihara, Toshi, and James R. Holmes. *Red Star Over the Pacific: China's Rise & the Challenge to U.S. Maritime Strategy* (Annapolis, Maryland: Naval University Press, 2010).

Index

About the Author

Sarwar A. Kashmeri is a Fellow of the Foreign Policy Association and adjunct professor of political science and applied research fellow at the Peace and War Center, Norwich University. He hosts Carnegie Corporation of New York's "China Focus" podcast series. Kashmeri is an author and current affairs commentator, noted for his expertise on U.S.-China relations, U.S.-Europe relations, and NATO. A former international businessman, he has served as a communications adviser to several Fortune 100 companies, and brings a global business perspective to his work in U.S. foreign policy and national security strategy. He served a four-year term as a nonresident Senior Fellow at the Atlantic Council's Brent Scowcroft Center on International Security. He earned a BS in aerospace engineering and an MS in engineering, both at Saint Louis University. His other published works include *NATO 2.0: Reboot or Delete?* (Potomac Books, 2011) and *America and Europe after 9/11 and Iraq: The Great Divide* (Praeger, 2006).